VW Beetle
Specification Guide 1949–1967

VW Beetle

Specification Guide 1949–1967

James Richardson

The Crowood Press

First published in 2007 by
The Crowood Press Ltd
Ramsbury, Marlborough
Wiltshire SN8 2HR

www.crowood.com

Paperback edition 2018

British Library Cataloguing-in-Publication Data
A catalogue record for this book is available from the British Library.

ISBN 978 1 78500 489 6

About the author
Richard Copping is Britain's most prolific author on matters Volkswagen, with well over twenty
books written about Beetles, Transporters, the VW Golf and more. His deep-rooted love for the
marque has encouraged him to amass a large collection of archive brochures, to travel the length
and breadth of the country visiting many of the Volkswagen enthusiast events, to photograph all
types of Volkswagen whenever the occasion arises and, above all, to write about the vehicles in a
style that has come to be recognized as both authoritative and lively.

Typeset and designed by D & N Publishing, Baydon, Wiltshire.

Printed and bound in India by Replika Press Pvt. Ltd.

contents

preface

The Volkswagen philosophy,1 January 1948 – 12 April 1968:

' … To develop one model of car to its highest technical excellence …to dedicate ourselves to the attainment of the highest quality,to destroy the notion that such high quality can only be obtained at high prices …   to give the car the highest value … to build it so that it retains that value …'

Heinz Nordhoff,Director General, 5 December 1961

Compared to the specification guides already published in this Crowood series – covering the VW Transporter and Microbus respectively, first in split-screen guise and then with the panoramic front window that led to the adoption of the 'Bay' nickname – this volume allocates a greater amount of space to the history of the product. The reason for this should soon become apparent. The cumulative production total of 1,833,000 for the Transporter manufactured between its debut in 1950 and the last days of July 1967 pales into insignificance when compared to that of Beetles produced during more or less the same period. One million such cars had left the Wolfsburg factory by August 1955, with a further million reached just over two years later during the last days of December 1957.By the end of 1967 and the period covered by this book, that total had risen to a figure well in excess of 10,000,000 cars.

Clearly with such volume, the Volkswagen Empire, which is what a once bombed-out ex-Nazi factory had become in the twenty-two years since the end of the war, had been created out of just one key model. Unusual in the extreme, sufficient space has to be allocated to the twenty years during which Volkswagen was ruled by Heinz Nordhoff.Why – unlike any other manufacturer – did Nordhoff fervently adhere to Ferdinand Porsche's pre-war design throughout his reign? Was the car truly irreplaceable? What special characteristics had the Beetle, which set it on the path to becoming the most produced single model ever? And if the years 1948 to 1968 are clearly worthy of analysis, so too must be Ferdinand Porsche's pre-war attempts to launch successfully a car for the people and the post-war military government's desire to rescue this symbol of the Nazi Party's bid for German supremacy in all aspects of life.

With the Beetle's place in Volkswagen's history duly assessed,only one problem presents itself.The specifications for the Beetles produced before the launch of the Deluxe,or Export, model in the summer of 1949 vary wildly according to the availability of raw materials and parts in the immediate post-war years.Inevitably then, the level of detail dedicated to Beetles of this vintage is less comprehensive than in later years.

No Beetle guide would be complete without the inclusion of the coveted convertible produced for Volkswagen by Karmann. Indeed, so integral was the model to the Beetle line-up from 1950 onwards, that in terms of specification it is included with the saloon in the year-by-year detail changes.With a soft-top always a part of Porsche's original plan and even something of a plaything for the British hierarchy, aside from the Karmann Cabriolet, space is allocated to the Radclyffe Roadster, Hebmüller coupé and other soft-top variants on the Beetle theme. For the curious, so too are some of the many coach-built models prevalent particularly in the 1950s. Sadly, space precludes more than passing reference to Volkswagen's own Beetle with a sporty body – the Karmann Ghia.

Writing about and listing details concerning the Beetle is always a pleasure, for it is through this car that my general appreciation of all types of Volkswagen – including modern day water-cooled models – arose. That interest has extended further to include sales literature and other memorabilia – some of which are used in this volume. I trust that you will find this volume an invaluable comprehensive guide to Beetleology.

Richard Copping, 2007

1

the KdF-Wagen

Two KdF-Wagens that have survived! The one bearing the number 98 is resident in Germany, the other travelled from the USA to Germany via England in 1999 to attend a classic Volkswagen event held at Bad Camberg.

FERDINAND PORSCHE AND THE *VOLKSAUTO*

Throughout his working life, one of Ferdinand Porsche's passions was to design and build a *Volksauto* – a small car for the people. While in the employ of others, including Austro-Daimler and Daimler-Motoren AG, albeit for many years at director level – his ambition could be and was readily quashed. In what of necessity is a gross simplification of Porsche's career, by 1931 the highly talented, yet equally volatile,

designer had parted company with so many manufacturers that there remained little option for him but to set up his own bureau. With the only constraint now placed upon him being one of available funds, he was able to pursue his small car story with renewed vigour.

Labelling his small car as Project 12, what started to emerge was a vehicle that bore more than a passing resemblance to an insect when compared to conventional cars of the time. Planned to incorporate four-wheel independent suspension and to be light enough

in weight for a low-horsepower engine to be sufficient, the backbone of the car was a tunnel along the front-to-rear centreline.

Fritz Neumeyer of the Zündapp Works, having already expressed more than a passing interest in developing a small car to supplement his motorcycle activities, heard of Porsche's project and commissioned him to develop it further. The Zündapp *Volksauto* was duly born, the only significant difference between it and Porsche's original concept being a water-cooled five-cylinder radial engine. Sadly, when put on test, the progress of the prototype aluminium over a wooden-frame-bodied car was disastrous. Engines boiled and Porsche's patent torsion bars shattered. When Neumeyer realized just how costly the stamping presses required to make the final shaped steel body parts would be, he decided to call a halt and paid Porsche off accordingly.

Later in 1931, Porsche was approached by Fritz von Falkenhayn, head of the NSU *Motorwerks*. He too wanted a small car and by 1933 Porsche had engineered the original Project 12 design to resemble something even closer to the form the Beetle would take a few years later. Amongst this vehicle's key attributes was a 1.5ltr air-cooled flat-four engine capable of 116km/h (72mph), while the body was shapelier than that of the Zündapp project car. Sadly, Porsche was to be thwarted once more when von Falkenhayn received a letter from the managing director of Fiat, reminding him of an agreement signed in 1930, whereby he had contracted to cease car production both then and in the future, Fiat in reality having bought the NSU operation.

FATE PLAYS HER HAND

Speaking at the Berlin Motor Show in February 1933, the newly appointed Chancellor, Adolf Hitler, spoke of the urgent need to see Germany motorized.

Highlighting a programme of road building (the *autobahns*), the rest of Hitler's speech lay mostly in the direction of motor sport, but nevertheless the requirement for a small car suitable for the masses was highlighted. As a result, Porsche spent the rest of 1933 preparing his now famous *Exposé*, in which he outlined the ideal specification for the kind of car of which Hitler had spoken. His paper was presented to the Transport Ministry on 17 January 1934, just a short time before the next Berlin Motor Show.

The historical significance of Porsche's *Exposé* cannot be underrated. In his introduction, Porsche stressed that to date, manufacturers' attempts to produce a car for the people had lacked the necessary ingredient of a low selling price, while their efforts had been targeted at a limited market. The only solution was to place the development of a people's car in the hands of the state – the benefits being the inclusion of the technical prowess of the nation's youth, plus its pivotal role in the stimulation of the economy as a whole.

The volkswagen, Porsche insisted, should not be a scaled-down replica of a larger car – with a consequent loss in dimensions, power and weight. For its success, it had to be a complete and fully practical car, yet also capable of competing with any other model. Porsche's definition of the volkswagen encompassed five key points:

1. The volkswagen should be a functional vehicle of normal dimensions but of relatively low weight. The use of fundamentally new processes would achieve this goal.
2. The volkswagen had to be readily capable of normal maximum speeds and climbing capabilities.
3. The volkswagen must be fully functional with a comfortable amount of space for its passengers.
4. The volkswagen should not be a vehicle limited in its possible uses. By a simple exchange of bodywork the passenger car could be transformed into either a commercial vehicle or one suitable for certain military purposes.
5. The volkswagen should not be unnecessarily complex – but rather as far as possible should be foolproof, leading to an absolute minimum in servicing costs.

Porsche's acceptability criteria:

- the best possible suspension and handling
- a maximum speed of around 100km/h (62mph)
- a climbing capability of in the region of 30 per cent
- a four-seater enclosed body
- the lowest possible purchase price, coupled to equally economical running costs.

With a whole series of specially posed shots advertising the merits of KdF-Wagen ownership, an endorsement from the Führer seated in the convertible version of the car and stylish artwork, the early brochures were well-thought-out sales tools.

Porsche proceeded to list the volkswagen's key specifications, which included a track of 1,200mm (46.8in), a wheelbase of 2,500mm (97.5in), an engine producing a maximum of 26bhp at 3,500rpm, a kerb weight of 650kg (1,433lb) and a selling price of 1,550RM (roughly equal to the cheapest options from other German manufacturers). He duly recommended that the government hand the project over to him, providing the necessary funding to design, build and test one car. Should the volkswagen prove successful, the state would recommend that the 'industry' put it into production, with Porsche receiving royalty payments for any of his patents incorporated into the car.

Porsche's appendices elaborated on what was to become a very familiar specification and included each wheel being independently sprung, the use of his patent torsion bars, an air-cooled four-cylinder, four-stroke engine (or an air-cooled radial three-cylinder, two-stroke engine), separate bodyshell and a chassis consisting of two parallel longitudinal tubes running centrally, plus parallel lateral tubes.

RESISTANCE TO THE VOLKSWAGEN SUPPRESSED

Although the sequence of events around the time of the publication of Porsche's *Exposé* is unclear, what remains certain is that Jakob Werlin visited the designer, which in turn led to a meeting between Hitler and Porsche. Porsche knew Werlin through his years at Daimler-Benz, while Hitler's acquaintance with the salesman had been initiated when the Nazi leader bought his first car, a Mercedes, from Werlin in 1923. Porsche hastened to Berlin and the hotel Kaiserhof to discuss his volkswagen, or so he thought, with Werlin. Hitler had quite definite ideas regarding a car for the people and manhandled the course of the meeting accordingly. He wanted four-wheel drive, a 30bhp, three-cylinder, air-cooled diesel engine, which would also be suitable for military use. As for the price – it must fall below the magical 1,000RM figure.

Shortly afterwards, the RDA – the Reichsverband der Automobilindustrie, or the German car manufacturers' trade association – was informed that Hitler wished to progress the development of Porsche's volkswagen. The RDA's contract with Porsche was 'to further the motorization of the German people on the basis of cooperative action and by enlisting the best talents of German car manufacture'.

Der KdF-Wagen von A bis Z was an elaborate manual containing all the information required by a potential owner of a KdF-Wagen. Cleverly designed, the centrefold, featuring a ghosted illustration of the KdF-Wagen, encouraged readers to find out more about each aspect of the car, by using carefully colour-coded cut-outs at the edge of the double page.

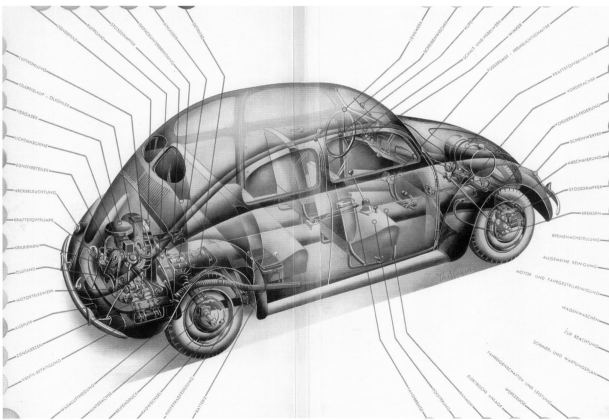

The V3 series – this is the V3/2 parked in Porsche's garden – dated from 1936 and although recognizable as a forerunner of the KdF-Wagen and Beetle, tests and trials led to many design changes.

Following the V3 series, the W30 series – dating from 1936 to 1938 – still looked noticeably different from the final product. These were the cars that were rigorously tested over many, many miles. Rearward visibility was extremely limited, while the knuckle-scraping boot lid and 'suicide' doors were two more features to be redesigned.

Years later, another key player in the Beetle's story, Heinz Nordhoff – at the time Opel's representative on the RDA – was to say that, 'Porsche led a fight against the entire German car industry … a secret underground fight of course and one which ended to his and the volkswagen's benefit only because Hitler stood behind the entire plan'.

At the 1935 Berlin Motor Show, Hitler sounded optimistic regarding progress with the people's car. He spoke of preliminary design work having already been completed and plans to test the first models by the middle of the year. Reality was somewhat different and twelve months later Hitler had little option but to repeat the same story once more.

Nevertheless, from V1 and V2 to the V3, W30, V303, VW38 and VW39, the car we know today as the Beetle gradually emerged. Starting as a vehicle without a rear window and featuring a tiny knuckle-scraping boot lid, headlamps fixed to the lower and unopenable section of the bonnet, and suicide doors, it was only after considerable testing of the car's mechanical abilities that the body progressed significantly. The VW38, which made its debut at the beginning of 1938, was the first prototype to feature the characteristic split-rear window – although this was more a matter of practicality than design, as at the time the curved glass required to produce a single window at the car's rear could not be produced. No car was tested as rigorously as the volkswagen. The W30 series of thirty cars, for example, driven by 120 seconded SS troops, amassed a total of 2.4 million km on their combined test runs. Ferry Porsche, eventually to become head of the Porsche operation after the war, was already involved with the volkswagen project and was later to comment that 'this was the first time in Europe that as many as thirty test cars had been used by a manufacturer'. The result was a car that was ahead of its time, uniquely efficient, serviceable, yet carrying a low initial cost – all prerequisites of the people's car as far as Hitler was concerned.

The initial reaction to the earlier prototypes by members of the RDA was predictable, as it declared the volkswagen to be extremely ugly, while also straying almost beyond the boundaries of acceptable convention. Although the RDA was wise enough to recommend continuation of the project, it also made the suggestion that all German automobile manufacturers should be invited to take part in a competition to find the very best design for any further development. Perhaps inevitably, it was only a short time after this that all files relating to the volkswagen had to be handed over to the Transport Ministry, while an order passed in the *Reichstag* established control over both iron and steel. The days of any rival volksauto were strictly limited! When Opel offered to cut the price of its own people's car – the P4 – from 1,450 to 1,250RM it was made clear – albeit unofficially – that such a move would not be tolerated, as no German manufacturer would be allowed to produce a vehicle approaching the price of the volkswagen.

In late May 1937 the Nazi-owned Gesellschaft zur Vorbereitung des Volkswagens – or the Volkswagen Development Company – was formed. Its board of management consisted of Porsche, Jakob Werlin and Dr Bodo Lafferentz, who was the chief aid to the boss of the German Labour Front (DAF – Deutsche Arbeiterfront), Robert Ley. With capital of 480,000RM at its disposal initially, Porsche could push ahead at a pace unheard of previously.

A PURPOSE-BUILT FACTORY FOR THE VOLKSWAGEN

Bodo Lafferentz was the member of the Volkswagen Development Company charged with locating a site suitable for a Volkswagen factory. His brief required finding land of around 20 sq miles (51.8 sq km) in size, with a proximity to transportation facilities and appropriately close to supplies of raw materials, without being too near to the country's western boundaries. After thorough searching, Lafferentz chanced upon the land surrounding Schloss Wolfsburg, the home of Count Werner von der Schulenburg and conveniently close to the Mittelland Canal. Although the Count enlisted the help of numerous experts to fight his corner – including a specialist in the field of rare mosquitoes – papers transferring the land to the state were drawn up in January 1938 and duly signed. The fact that the Nazis had decided that they must have a purpose-built factory and associated township for their volkswagen's construction

proved crucial to the Beetle's survival after the war.

Hitler laid the foundation stone of the volkswagen factory on 26 May 1938. Apart from the volkswagen saloon, both a convertible version and a sunroof model were on display. Hitler's speech demonstrated clearly why he hadn't countenanced opposition to the volkswagen project:

> When I came to power in 1933, I saw one problem that had to be tackled at once – the problem of motorization. In this sphere, Germany was behind everyone else. The output of private cars in Germany had reached the laughable figure of 46,000 a year. The first step towards putting an end to this was to do away with the idea that a motor car is an article of luxury …

Although Hitler's surprise name for the volkswagen – announced at the foundation-stone-laying ceremony – 'horrified' Porsche and anyone with an interest in selling the car anywhere other than in Nazi-controlled Germany, its use helps to distinguish the pre-war volkswagen from the post-conflict attempt to provide transport for Allied personnel and the meteoric rise of the Beetle under Heinz Nordhoff. Hitler concluded his foundation-laying speech with the following words: 'This car shall carry the name of the organization which works hardest to provide the broad masses of our people with joy and, therefore,

strength. It shall be called the KdF-Wagen!' ('Strength-through-joy, a subsidiary movement within DAF responsible for leisure-time activities.')

SELLING THE KDF-WAGEN

The KdF-Wagen factory was designed by its architect to be 1 mile (1.6 km) in length and to include a tall administration building. A structure on this scale was essential if Hitler's demands were to be fulfilled. Robert Ley, head of the German Labour Front, reported that it was 'the Führer's will that within a few years no fewer than 6,000,000 volkswagens' would be occupying German roads. Even more extravagantly, Ley predicted that 'in ten years' time there will be no working person in Germany who does not own a people's car'. Although, as events were to prove, this was totally unrealistic, the Volkswagen Development Company set targets for KdF-Wagen production even before the factory was built. From the modest 400 cars to be manufactured during the last two months of 1938, by December 1939 it was planned to be building 10,000 KdF-Wagens per month, rising to a yearly production of 450,000 by 1944.

Here was a people's car unprecedented then – but there was one major obstacle to ownership even when availability was ignored. Hitler had demanded of Porsche that the KdF-Wagen be built and sold at a price of 900RM against the designer's *Exposé* proposal

The VW 38s, in both Saloon and Saloon with sunroof guise, were paraded around Germany after the factory foundation-laying ceremony and received a genuinely enthusiastic response.

Always planned as part of the KdF-Wagen series, this Cabriolet dating from 1938 looks not that dissimilar to the early Karmann examples, which would follow some twelve years later.

of 1,500RM. The average German's savings in 1934 had fallen below 1,000RM, while Hitler stressed that 'it must be possible to make the German people a gift of a motor vehicle which will not cost more than they have hereto been accustomed to paying for a medium-priced motor cycle and whose petrol consumption will be low'.

Although by the time of the factory foundation-stone-laying ceremony the cost of the KdF-Wagen had risen to a basic price of 990RM at the factory, hidden extra costs such as insurance and delivery took the price well over the 1,000RM barrier. The Nazis' answer to this predicament was the now famous, if somewhat draconian, Savings Scheme. At a rate of 5RM per week, it would take a saver a total of four years and seven months to amass the required 1,190RM, and then the person would only become eligible for a car, with a possible wait of up to a further five years to acquire a KdF-Wagen. Nevertheless, a total of 336,688 Germans eventually signed up to the scheme, although not a single one received a KdF-Wagen.

The issue of price is undoubtedly a further factor in the Beetle's post-war survival and success story. Every cost-cutting step had been taken – without compromising standards. This was a people's car without equal.

END GAME FOR THE NAZIS

Although a small number of KdF-Wagens were built as the war progressed, Porsche's attention was diverted to military versions of his protégé. From the *Kübelwagen* and the amphibious *Schwimmwagen*, to KdF-bodied vehicles with Kübel running gear, none concern us here. Nor does the fate of Porsche after the war – for he was out of the Beetle's story. Only one wartime issue is of importance – the survival of the KdF factory, for without it, its post-war occupants would have had no reason to be present and hence to turn their attention to the Beetle.

A number of variations on the KdF-Wagen theme were built during the war, although numbers were comparatively small. Porsche and his colleagues meanwhile concentrated their efforts on both the Kübelwagen and Schwimmwagen.

March 1946 – with Ivan Hirst at the wheel, the factory celebrated meeting its target of producing 1,000 cars in a month.

The **1000th** VOLKSWAGEN built during MARCH 1946 coming from Assembly Line

2 the Wolfsburg Motor Works

THE ROUTE TO BRITISH CONTROL

Although a defeated Hitler didn't commit suicide until 30 April 1945 (with Admiral Dönitz's official surrender following on 7 May), the war effectively ended at the KdF-Stadt over two days – 10 and 11 April 1945 – with the arrival of American forces.

In the death-rattle weeks of the Third Reich, some of the factory's machinery had been despatched to the Longwy mineshafts on the Belgium–Luxembourg border. Fortunately, the chief inspector at the KdF plant managed to persuade Ferdinand Porsche to stop this practice and simply hide equipment in the township or the factory itself. Other items were stored locally and these included front ends and steering parts, which were stored in the village of Fallersleben, and engines, which were taken to a potato dehydration plant at Neinfort. Had everything been shipped off to Longwy, the factory would have been devoid of machine tools, making it impossible to restart vehicle production.

Closer still to the end of the war, the acting Mayor of KdF-Stadt was informed by factory personnel that they had been instructed to blow up the power station and the canal bridges. Fortunately, the Mayor's protests that the generators were essential as the town's only source of electricity were heeded. This action was another decisive factor in the factory's post-war survival story.

Although it was the Americans who 'rescued' the factory and associated township, both Fallersleben and the now unnamed plant lay in the British Zone of Occupation. During May 1945, the Americans gradually handed it over to the British. A survey of the damaged factory revealed that the parts of it left unscathed after bombing raids had been looted, while the cellars were flooded thanks to a combination of bomb craters and cracked foundations. In total, nearly 55 per cent of the factory was affected to some degree by Allied action, with 20.2 per cent totally destroyed, 13.6 per cent heavily damaged and the remainder – 20.9 per cent – having suffered relatively superficial harm. However, thanks to the Mayor, the power station remained operational. A unit of the Royal Electrical and Mechanical Engineers (REME) was despatched to the former KdF factory, where it set up a repair facility for British army vehicles. In August 1945 a Yorkshireman, Major Ivan Hirst, was sent to the factory with no specific orders other than to take control. Nevertheless, the days of a nameless plant with no purpose were over – the factory and surrounding township became Wolfsburg.

Major Ivan Hirst, who was Senior Resident British Officer from August 1945 and, despite his personal modesty, the man generally credited as the driving force behind the Beetle's reincarnation after the war.

THE FACTORY'S FATE

After the war the German armaments industry was to be completely dismantled and any building associated with such deeds demolished, while all countries that had been at war against Germany could bid for both machine tools and capital equipment as war reparations. The Volkswagen factory, despite its involvement in war work – particularly 'V' weapon development and production – was accepted as a building genuinely constructed for the purpose of manufacturing cars and thus spared demolition. However, a complication arose, as under the 'Level of Industry Plan for Germany' any factory not operational in 1938 was deemed to have been built as part of Germany's war effort and therefore surplus to requirements. Quotas had been set for each zone of occupation and vehicle production in the British zone was entirely taken care of by Ford. As a result, Wolfsburg was subject to war reparations.

Regarding ownership, Volkswagenwerk GmbH was wholly owned by the German Labour Front, itself an integral part of the Nazi Party, which had been abolished in its entirety by the Allies immediately upon Germany's surrender. Officially ownerless, nevertheless the factory still existed as a private limited company in law and was therefore brought within the Control Branch of the Control Commission Finance Division.

From this very shaky position, Hirst and his colleagues set in place a course of action that saved both the factory and the Beetle, whilst sowing the seeds for what was to become a hallmark of post-war Germany's economic revival.

NECESSARY TRANSPORT

Before the war, Colonel Michael McEvoy, who was based at Rhine Army headquarters, had 'road-tested' the KdF-Wagen at the Berlin Motor Show of 1939. Suitably impressed then, he now had the idea of resurrecting the wartime military version of the car, as much needed transport for the occupying forces, but without cost to the British taxpayer or economy.

McEvoy's idea came to nothing due to a deal struck by Ferdinand Porsche in 1938. While on a visit to the United States, Porsche had met with the Budd

Corporation and acquired the rights to manufacture the all-steel body of the KdF-Wagen using Budd techniques under licence. In return, it was agreed that should the Volkswagenwerk produce a new variation on the KdF-Wagen saloon theme – at the time assumed to be a Cabriolet – the Ambi Budd factory in Berlin would build the bodies. As a result, when the first variation proved to be the military usage Kübelwagen, it was this vehicle's body that was manufactured in Berlin. By the end of the war, the Ambi Budd factory had suffered so much bomb damage that only a few Kübel dies remained; also, in the division of Germany by the Allies, it was situated in the non-cooperative Soviet sector of the city. Clearly, there was no realistic chance of resuming Kübel production in any shape or form.

Ivan Hirst turned his attention to the saloon, a wartime example of which was found at the factory awaiting repair. He had the car refurbished and painted khaki before despatching it to Rhine Army headquarters, where McEvoy demonstrated the Beetle with consummate skill. The positive reaction was such that in September 1945 the Military Government placed an order for 20,000 such cars, all for the armed forces or official usage. Manufacture started in late 1945 with a recorded 1,785 cars – many of which utilized the Kübelwagen's chassis – being successfully produced by the end of the year in the most adverse conditions. Apart from factors like a missing press-shop roof and the lack of a consistent supply of parts and components, persons key to the operation were regularly dismissed, as their former affiliations to the Nazis became known.

A total of 10,020 Beetles left Wolfsburg in 1946 – a figure still short of the Government's initial order, but there was nevertheless due celebration when the ten-thousandth Beetle to be produced under British custodianship emerged on 14 October of the same year. Ivan Hirst loved to recall those early post-war days at Wolfsburg. One of his recollections serves to show the inbuilt ingenuity he carried to overcome all obstacles to production. At one stage, only three weeks' stock of carburettors remained. As Pierburg in Berlin made these under licence from Solex, it was apparent that no further stocks would be forthcoming for

some time. Hirst stripped one of the remaining carburettors down, dividing the parts into those that might be manufactured within the Wolfsburg complex and those that couldn't. He then proceeded to enlist the services of a camera firm in nearby Brunswick to make the precision parts in brass.

REJECTION LEADING TO GREATER THINGS

Country after country turned down both Wolfsburg and its 'ugly and noisy' car as an option to advance their own motoring aspirations. Henry Ford II, for example, saw the proximity of the plant to the Russian Zone on a map and immediately rescinded his declared interest, while the Australian Reparations Commission was deterred from transferring the plant in its entirety to Australia when it learned of the four-year reserve placed upon it. Britain's Society of Motor Manufacturers and Traders meanwhile commissioned a series of technical assessments, which not only were considerably less than complimentary regarding the Beetle's assets, but also led to calls for the factory to be broken up. William Rootes – perhaps the most condemnatory of all – advised Hirst on a visit to the factory that, 'if you think you are going to get cars made here, you are a bloody fool!'

Hirst and his team persisted, introducing, for example, a service and parts manual for the car, while painstakingly endeavouring to rectify defects and improve quality. As 1947 progressed it became increasingly obvious that, despite its detractors, the Beetle had a future. Orders continued to grow, while the first tentative steps were taken to export the Beetle.

However, as the threat of war reparations began to disappear and other obstacles diminished, the reality of Hirst's position became increasingly evident. It was not and never had been the intention that the British would manage the Volkswagen plant on a long-term basis. The German custodian, Hermann Munch, was a Berlin lawyer with little experience in any relevant field. Someone with an appropriate knowledge had to be found not only to take charge, but also to drive Volkswagen forwards. That man turned out to be an ex-Opel man, one Heinz Nordhoff.

3

the Nordhoff years

*Heinz Nordhoff,
Director General
1948–68.*

INTERPRETING HISTORY

For many years now, it has been fashionable to criticize Volkswagen's Director General of twenty years' standing, Heinz Nordhoff (1948–68), as a blinkered individual obsessed by one car to the detriment of the company's long-term well-being. Recent literature produced by Volkswagen's 'Corporate History Department' serves to perpetuate this view of the company's progress as the 1950s merged into the following decade. Writing of the situation at the time of Nordhoff's death in April 1968, Volkswagen's designated historian, Markus Lupa, felt honour-bound to declare that 'VW's main competitive advantage – the mass production of one model – now threatened to become an ominous disadvantage'. While acknowledging that Nordhoff had grown the business from a mere trifle to a position at 'the pinnacle of the European automobile industry', Lupa considered that 'far-reaching changes were necessary … in order to maintain this position'. The clear implication is that the corporate line remains one of condemning Nordhoff for not replacing the Beetle part-way through his tenure of office.

Needless to say, not all observers share the opinions expressed by Volkswagen. To some at least, Nordhoff

neither perpetuated a one-model policy, nor left the company in a position requiring radical changes on his death. No other operation had so successfully penetrated worldwide markets, while the hard-headed Nordhoff – a businessman through and through – would have been the first to abandon the Beetle if there had been serious signs of it losing its vice-like grip on worldwide small car sales. The introduction of the larger saloon – the VW 1500 – at the point when production of the Beetle finally showed signs of catching up with ever-increasing demand, demonstrated prudence in satisfying customer expectations of Beetle availability and an eagerness to develop a range when the opportunity arose. The advent of a still larger family car and variant – the 411, developed in Nordhoff's lifetime but launched after his death – further indicated his readiness to move with the times. His willingness to replace the much-loved and highly successful first-generation Transporter with a new and better model in the summer of 1967, at the same point as the updated Beetle was relaunched, demonstrates a lack of

LEFT: Initially, Volkswagen's publicity material relied on black and white photography. This item, dating from 1950 and produced for the home market, gives equal priority to the Export and Standard model (depicted here).

The commissioning of the highly talented artist Bernd Reuters led to stylized images of the Beetle dominating Volkswagen's publicity for the best part of a decade. The cover and centre pages depicted here can be dated to the period between October 1952 and March 1953. Reuters highlights all the improvements made to Beetles produced in the last months of the split rear screen with simple sketches.

sentimentality for once-potent but latterly outdated products.

Without Nordhoff, just as without Porsche, Hitler and Hirst, the Beetle wouldn't have become the world's most popular car. Nordhoff is no misguided villain of the Volkswagen story.

NORDHOFF'S APPOINTMENT AND BACKGROUND

Nordhoff was born in 1899. His first job after completing his studies at Berlin Technical College was as an aero-engine designer at BMW. Three years later, in 1930, he joined Opel, which had recently been acquired by General Motors. His potential acknowledged, he was despatched to the USA to discover Detroit's approach to production techniques. In 1936 he became a Director at Opel, while during the war he was put in charge of the company's Brandenburg lorry factory, which was the largest in Europe at the time. Although never a supporter of the Nazi cause, for his services to the Reich he was awarded the minor honour of *Wehrwirtschafts-führer*, the result of which was to make

him unemployable in the US-controlled and Opel-based sector after the war. His only remaining option was to manage a small garage and repair shop, courtesy of the widow of a friend who owned an Opel dealership.

It was from this position that Nordhoff joined Volkswagen. While it has already been stated that the British needed someone capable of running Volkswagen on a long-term basis, the circumstances of Nordhoff's appointment need clarification. The factory's German custodian, Hermann Munch, did not have an industry background and this often caused Ivan Hirst and his colleagues additional problems. Hirst spoke to his superior officer, Colonel Radclyffe, making a good case for the appointment of an experienced number two to Munch. Through a contact in Hamburg, Hirst learnt of Nordhoff. Invited to Wolfsburg, Nordhoff so impressed Hirst that according to legend he was unable to 'recommend' the German for the job he had been interviewed for, resulting in Nordhoff packing his bags and making to depart. After a suitable pause, Hirst informed Nordhoff that he

was proposing him for the position of Director General. Nordhoff started work on 1 January 1948, with Munch departing on 30 April of the same year. Hirst's role changed too, as his main purpose in the remaining time he spent at Wolfsburg was simply to monitor Nordhoff's performance and to serve as a fallback should the new Director General have to leave due to political pressures. As for Nordhoff, his only stipulation before agreeing to join Volkswagen was that he would not tolerate any interference. Again, legend has it that the question was asked whether this included the British, to which the reply was that it meant the British first of all.

NORDHOFF AND THE BEETLE

Although loosely involved with the early Beetle prototypes before the war – thanks to his position as an Opel delegate with the RDA – Nordhoff had never set foot in Wolfsburg, nor driven a Beetle before his appointment as Director General and was startled to discover that the Volkswagen had 'more flaws than a

From 1953–57 most brochures featured this illustration on their covers. Inside, Reuters modernized his images, as changes were made to the cars, while also varying the paintwork colour from year to year.

The cover of this brochure dating from 1959 reveals a classic Reuters ploy. The occupants of the car are smaller than reality, giving the impression that the Beetle is particularly spacious and comfortable.

dog has fleas'. Apart from its ugly duckling appearance, the car was both noisy and badly sprung, while the upholstery and paint finish left much to be desired. Crucially, engine life was unacceptably short.

However, the Director General, who spent the first six months of his appointment camped in a room adjacent to his office, in order that he could devote all his attentions to the matters in hand, was soon talking of 'unlimited possibilities' and the 'special personality' of the car. The Beetle, he believed, 'had definite features which were greatly desirable and not found in cars of comparable size'.

Nordhoff openly stated that it was his 'life's aim to make this plant [Wolfsburg] into the greatest car factory in Europe'. His strategy to build his empire was three-fold: to make Beetle production not just financially viable but suitably profitable; to create a value-for-money product of the highest possible standard backed by first-class spares plus service facilities; and to generate the necessary income to be capable of becoming the symbol of Germany's post-war economic success through exports.

Of immediate concern was the number of hours – some 300 to 400 in total, nobody was quite sure – it took to build each car. Speaking in November 1958, Nordhoff reminded his audience that he:

had to start from scratch in the real sense of the word. 7,000 workers were painfully producing at the rate of a mere 6,000 cars a year – provided it did not rain too much. Most of the roof and all the windows of the factory had been destroyed. At this time, nearly three years after the end of the war, 109.6 men were required to produce one car per day. Today this figure is 17.9.

Addressing the workforce just two months after he joined Volkswagen, Nordhoff insisted that, 'if we continue in this manner, we shall not continue for long. We must reach 100 hours per car'. Despite the initial reaction, which consisted of a mixture of incredulity and negativity, the workers reacted to the new spirit of urgency. By 1955, it took less than Nordhoff's goal of 100 hours to build a Beetle, while with unstoppable drive he had set in motion the process of increasing daily production as early as mid-1949. The decree went

out that 200 cars – compared to the previous 100 – would be built per day.

To Nordhoff's dismay, there was no cost-accounting system in place under the British. Not only were the costs of building a single Beetle unknown, but also it was apparent that one car might easily have cost considerably more or less than those immediately preceding or following it. Nordhoff quickly rectified this situation.

Of equal importance to both man-hours and cost was the issue of service. Hirst and the British had instigated a policy of both issuing maintenance guidelines and providing spares. Nordhoff turned both aspects into legends of the car-manufacturing world. Otto Höhne, once production chief at Volkswagen and a member of its *Vorstand*, credited Nordhoff with surveying world markets and planning a global service organization. 'No one had even thought that way before', he added. As for quality, the Director General appreciated that if the Beetle was to earn much-needed revenue from markets other than the home one, what was acceptable to a car-starved Germany would not be to the inhabitants of many other countries.

BELOW: Compare Reuters' image of the Cabriolet here with the white car reproduced on page 117 – a classic instance of reusing, or freshening, an illustration by giving both car and occupants a careful makeover. This brochure dates from 1960. Note, for example, how the sun visors have been revised in this, the later of the two publications.

RIGHT: Few brochures depict the rear end of a car, but Reuters was keen to remind would-be purchasers that, with effect from August 1957, the Beetle's rear window had grown considerably in size. This brochure cover is more often seen featuring a red Beetle.

'A FAVOURITE IN 136 COUNTRIES'

Come July 1949, an Export, or Deluxe, version of the Beetle was introduced, with production having started at the beginning of the previous month. Initially mechanically identical to the Beetle of old – a car now referred to as the Standard – the Export model featured a more upmarket trim package epitomized by ivory-coloured rather than black fittings, chrome replacing painted metal and, perhaps trivially, rear-seat bolster cushions.

The purpose of the Export model was exactly what it said on the label and Nordhoff was nothing if not persistent. His repeated attempts to penetrate the vast American market are recorded elsewhere in this volume, as are the eventual setting up of Beetle manufacturing and assembly satellites around the world. Key markets would include Brazil, South Africa, New Zealand, Australia and Mexico, plus inevitably every country in Europe, including the home of the small car – Great Britain.

Nordhoff's additional initial motive for export sales was to counteract the worst of a German winter, which was a time of low domestic market sales due to adverse weather conditions. His workforce was to be at maximum capacity at all times.

Out of the daily output of 1,280 Beetles produced in 1955, 700 were destined for export, while 400,000 of the million Beetles in existence by this time were in use in 103 countries in addition to the home market. With further expansion, a key marketing line for the Beetle in the 1960s came in the form of a question: 'Why is the Volkswagen a favourite in 136 countries? Because …'.

THE FIRST MILLION

The production survey contained in Chapter Four highlights the arrival of the millionth Beetle on 5 August 1955. This was an elaborate gold-painted affair, complete with diamante-encrusted bumpers. Although there had been celebrations when the five-hundred-

thousandth car rolled off the assembly line and would be again for the second, third and so on millionth vehicles – none would compare with the occasion of the first. Over 140,000 people attended the lengthy celebrations, including 1,000 international motoring journalists, one of whom was Bill Boddy, a British motoring writer, well-known for his passion at the time for the Beetle. Although perhaps the single most important event was the awarding of Nordhoff with Federal Germany's Distinguished Services Cross with Star and the Freedom of the City of Wolfsburg, for Beetle watchers, Boddy included, it was the Director General's speech that was of most interest.

If there had been any doubt about Nordhoff's passion for the product before, there could not be any longer. He reminded his audience that in 1948 there had been forty Beetle distributors in Germany and one abroad. By 1955 this had mushroomed to 1,000 in the home country and an astonishing 2,800 abroad. Nordhoff said that he

A typical Beetle dating from the period before the introduction of the Export model.

ABOVE: Two contemporary, exceptionally well-known publicity shots of the new Export model – the Deluxe Beetle.

LEFT: This Maroon Red (L55) Export model dates from 1952, but was built before October of that year, as evidenced by the lack of trim inserts around the windows and by the grooved bumper.

The Black Cabriolet with optional Ivory paintwork on the side panels was manufactured before October 1952.
The bumpers, style of tail light and circular trims near the base of both front wings help to date the car.

could claim the best sales and service in Europe and no feeling of inferiority when compared to organizations of a similar nature in America.

Boddy reported that Nordhoff was immensely proud to say that:

> for sixty-five years there has been a European automobile industry and connected with it are names having an historical ring; but to pass the millionth production mark for the first time in Europe since the end of the war with one and the same type of car has been reserved for one of its youngest factories, the Volkswagenwerk.

His determination to advance both Volkswagen and the Beetle still further was demonstrated in his concluding remarks: 'Hard work and determination has always been a strong point of the Germans, for we enjoy if we know for what purpose …'. The purpose was indeed clear for all to see.

This Standard Model Oval dates from before August 1955, as indicated by
heart-shaped tail lights and a single tailpipe.

BEETLE SUPPLY AND DEMAND

After an initial struggle, by 1955 Nordhoff could say that 'the American public like our cars'. His main task became one of taking 'the necessary steps before making our preliminary plans for 1956 to ensure that she [the USA] will get them'. Thanks to a dynamic new style of advertising initiated in 1959, courtesy of the Doyle Dane Bernbach agency, the Beetle soon became a cult car in America, further increasing demand for Volkswagens. From the 279,986 cars produced in 1955, within five short years that figure had more than doubled. In 1960 Volkswagen produced 739,443 Beetles. Nordhoff's ongoing challenge was to attempt to meet the demand for his product with an appropriate supply.

As the 1950s progressed Wolfsburg was supported by a bevy of additional factories. On 8 March 1956 Transporter production transferred to a brand-new factory constructed in Hanover, partly to ease the pressure on Wolfsburg. In July 1958 a former aircraft engine plant at Kassal was acquired, with the purpose of repairing, expanding and modernizing it to accommodate Volkswagen's axle production, while looking after the reconditioning of engines. The smaller factory at Brunswick grew, while Wolfsburg itself was extended.

Nordhoff summarized Volkswagen's very necessary expansion in a speech made in Switzerland in March 1960. Referring to what had always been a disparity between available cars and increasing demand for them, Nordhoff spoke of his actions to 'normalize the relationship':

> In 1959 we invested 500 million DM and boosted production by 1,000 Volkswagens to 3,000 per day. In 1960, we once again invested 5,000 million DM and in January boosted production by 100 VWs per day. In February, by another 100 per day, and in March, once again by 100 per day. By the end of 1960 we shall produce 4,000 Volkswagens daily. Then we believe we shall have reached a balance between supply and demand, so that we can finally deliver Volkswagens to customers without a waiting period …

MODEL POLICY

An extract from Nordhoff's speech made in November 1958, when he received the prestigious American Elmer A. Sperry medal for his and Ferdinand Porsche's contribution to transportation, clearly outlines why the Beetle remained at the forefront throughout his twenty years as Director General:

I brushed away all of the temptations to change model and design. In any sound design there are almost unlimited possibilities – and this certainly was a sound one. I see no sense in starting anew every few years with the same teething troubles, making obsolete almost all the past. I went out on a limb. I took the chance of breaking away from the beaten path and of doing something unusual but highly constructive for transport-hungry Europe – and not Europe alone.

Offering people an honest value, a product of the highest quality, with low original cost and incomparable value, appealed more to me than being driven around by a bunch of hysterical stylists trying to sell people something they really do not want to have. And it still does! Improving quality and value steadily, without increasing price … building a product of which I and every other Volkswagen worker can be truly proud … these things are, in my opinion, an engineer's task.

… I am firmly convinced that there will always be a market in this world, which we are far from covering now, for simple, economical and dependable transportation and for an honest value in performance and quality. I am convinced that, all over the world … there are millions of people who will gladly exchange chromium-plated gadgets and excessive power for economy, long life and inexpensive maintenance.

So I have decided to stick to the policy that has served us so well. Based on Professor Porsche's original design, the Volkswagen of today looks almost exactly like the prototype model that was produced twenty years ago, but every single part of this car has been refined and improved over the years – these will continue to be our 'model changes'. This policy has required, of course, a great deal in the way of determination and courage, on the part of myself and the members of our organization. But it has led to success, and there is no greater justification than success …

Other speeches made and interviews given by Nordhoff relayed exactly the same message. In 1957, he reminded the German service organization that in the early days of his management 'everyone was saying that the shape [of the Beetle] must be changed as quickly as possible, because the car could never succeed with such an outmoded style. The shape remained.' Nordhoff continued:

It is my firm conviction that sticking to what we have is one of the most important elements of our success. But year by year, a fresh wave of rumours appears: there is going to be a new Volkswagen. Can anybody seriously believe that we would change this car, which has scored so many successes? You can rest assured that I shall not make this mistake.

ABOVE: Later Oval model Beetles, those built after July 1955 for the '56 and '57 model years, can be identified by twin tailpipes and larger tail lights mounted higher up on the wings.
BELOW: Although this split-window Beetle is host to a number of accessories, it can be dated to the period between October 1952 and March 1953 by its tail-light design, the plain and sturdy bumpers and the brightwork inserts around the car's windows.

This, the cover from the last brochure to feature the artwork of Bernd Reuters, depicts the new 1961 model – the 34bhp Beetle. Despite the new or reworked drawings, the era of implying the Beetle was something it could never be – a spacious, yet sportily fast car – was rapidly drawing to a close.

We shall concentrate on eradicating gradually and positively all those small and large design errors inevitable in any car and this is what we are doing.

On viewing one of the various prototypes he commissioned to ensure the Beetle could not be bettered, Nordhoff's summary of his reasons for its rejection confirms his philosophy.

If you make a car 50cm longer, you add 100 kilos to the weight. That means higher fuel consumption straight away. But most of all you need a bigger engine and that takes you straight into a higher price bracket. As long as our product sells as well as it does at present, it is wiser and more economical to go on developing it.

Antagonized in late 1959 by an interviewer from the German magazine *Der Spiegel* who accused him of clinging on to a twenty-five-year-old design until such time that 'the market tramples it underfoot', Nordhoff was at his most scathing in his reply:

Do you think I have been asleep? What car is about to trample the Volkswagen underfoot? Of course, the day will come when we will build a new car, but I have already said that we are starting on the fourth million and then we will continue on to five. What does all this mean? Your question was, 'Why no new VW at the 1959 Motor Show?' My answer in brief was, because demand for this vehicle is so great, because not a single manufacturer in Europe can point to anything like three million satisfied owners of a single type … that is all I have to say on the matter.

Officially launched at the Frankfurt Motor Show in September 1961, some thought that Nordhoff had relented and was looking for his new car, the VW 1500, to be an eventual replacement for the Beetle, a fallacy perpetuated by some historians to this day. Contemporary literature produced by Volkswagen's marketing department indicates that the wily Director General had no such thoughts: 'Everybody knows the Volkswagen. Now, the new, larger VW 1500 is being introduced. The Volkswagen factory has no intention of replacing the renowned and successful Volkswagen. The VW 1500 is an addition to the range, resulting from an ever-increasing public demand for such a product.'

The 1960s for Nordhoff were no different than the previous decade. The demand for the Beetle was unrelenting – an additional model could only be

ABOVE AND RIGHT: *Beetles built after the July 1957–58 model year looked very different, as not only was there an increase in the size of the front screen, but also at the rear, where the change was particularly noticeable.*

LEFT AND BELOW LEFT: *The 1500 Beetle arrived as the top of the model range in August 1966 (1967 model year). Externally, the car changed little, with a new engine lid, designed to appease US officialdom. The new shape allowed the licence plate to sit nearer to vertical. The Zenith (pale) Blue car has won many awards in numerous Concours d'Elegance line-ups.*

ABOVE: *Although Beetles built after July 1960 sported a new, more powerful engine and many other changes, the only noticeable external change on European models was the appearance of wing-mounted front indicators, which replaced the semaphores of old.*

ABOVE: Despite the plaque indicating the year 1961, this Beetle dates from the 1962 model year – August 1961 to July 1962. Three-section tail lights were now part of the car's make-up, although in the previous year this had not been the case.

RIGHT: For the 1965 model year (August 1964), the size of the windows increased once more. While nowhere near as noticeable as in August 1957, the changes (particularly to the side windows) altered the character of the car.

BELOW: The 1966 model year (August 1965) saw the introduction of the 1300 Beetle. Externally, the car was indistinguishable from the previous year's model, except for a discreet 1300 badge on the engine lid.

ABOVE: The Cabriolet automatically acquired all the refinements bestowed upon the Saloon. For British enthusiasts, the early 1960s car pictured here is particularly well known, having been a regular at the shows for many years.

contemplated because, thanks to huge investment, at long last output and demand were more or less equal. The slogan perfected in the 1950s that '*Es lohnt sich, auf einen Volkswagen zu warten*' (A Volkswagen is worth waiting for) might at last have become redundant, but for Nordhoff the goal was still to continue on the road to perfection with the Beetle. Following a major revamp for the 1961 model year, which included a new 34bhp engine for the Beetle, larger windows appeared in August 1964, while a 1300cc engine was offered for the 1966 model year. Twelve months later, there was more power again – this time with a 1500 engine.

European-wide recession in the latter months of 1966 and the start of 1967 affected all car manufacturers badly and Volkswagen was no exception. Having taken the decision to criticize Government policy with regard to motoring, Nordhoff no doubt expected the backlash that came from the Finance Minister, Franz-Josef Strauss. He duly accused Nordhoff of producing too many Beetles – the wrong model and too few ideas. Nordhoff's response was to introduce a budget version of the Beetle, while ploughing ahead with his main purpose in life.

August 1967 saw the venerable split-screen Transporter banished from the Volkswagen range to be replaced by a new model, soon to be christened 'the Bay', thanks to its panoramic front window. Part of Volkswagen's planning process from 1964, the new Transporter proved once and for all that Nordhoff was entirely capable of replacing a product if he felt that its future was one of declining sales and a secondary position to that of rival manufacturers' products.

However, that Nordhoff was still entirely confident in the Beetle's long-term future as a viable sales asset is apparent in a speech he made in January 1968, just a few months before his death. At the time, the forty-plus-year-old design had just undergone a serious makeover, sufficient to warrant the marketing department to announce boldly on the front of the new model year brochures that here was '*Die neuen Käfer*', or '*The new Beetle*'. But, according to Nordhoff:

As an engineer who knows many cars and quite apart from the fact that I am a Volkswagen man, I would always rate the faithful Beetle as one of the happiest combinations amongst the automobiles of the world. You will understand me when I say very emphatically

Regular size. **Large economy size.**

Volkswagens come in two handy sizes: Sedan and Station Wagon.

The packages are very different, but the works are about the same.

There is a genuine Volkswagen engine in the back of each. It gives both cars solid traction on ice and snow.

The engines are air-cooled, too. So you never mess with water or anti-freeze.

The VW Sedan seats 4 adults comfortably or 5 adults uncomfortably. (A mother, a father and 3 kids are about right.)

The VW Wagon is only 9 inches longer than the Sedan, a neat trick all by itself.

It seats 8 comfortably, 9 uncomfortably and 10 very uncomfortably, but it's been

done. (The kids that fit are countless.)

The VW Sedan averages 32 miles to the gallon, the Wagon a mere 24.

Once upon a time, people had trouble deciding whether to buy a VW or not.

Now they have trouble deciding which size.

The US advertising agency Doyle, Dane, Bernbach (known as DDB) appointed by the VW boss in the USA at the time, Carl Hahn, revolutionized Volkswagen's advertising by offering one clear message per advert with accompanying no-nonsense – or even stark – imagery.

You're missing a lot when you own a Volkswagen.

A VW has fewer parts than other cars because it needs fewer parts.

It doesn't need a drive shaft to transfer engine power to the rear wheels. Because our car's engine is in back to start with (and to maintain traction with).

And it doesn't need a radiator, or a

water pump, or hoses. Because the engine's cooled with air, not water.

(When you drive your first VW, you may miss putting in antifreeze, rust inhibitors and whatnot. But you'll soon get used to it.)

The stuff a VW doesn't use, it doesn't have to haul (and waste gas on). Which

is one reason it averages 32 mpg.

And the parts you don't buy, you'll never repair. So you can't waste money on that.

Now you know why you can drive a VW for years and years with a lot of parts missing.

And never miss them.

ABOVE: A simple message of air-cooled reliability expressed in an eye-catching and witty way.

BELOW: The cover of this 1965 Beetle brochure demonstrates DDB's effect as the years passed. Stunning photography and particularly clever wording – a far cry from the often turgid text of the 1950s.

that the star of the Beetle is still shining with undiminished brightness and you see for yourselves every day what vitality there is hidden in this car which has been pronounced dead more often than all of these designs of which hardly a memory remains. I am absolutely sure that our Beetle will be produced for a very long time to come.

The year of Nordhoff's death saw the highest ever number of Beetles at some 390,000 cars exported to America, while overall production in 1968 stood at 1,136,134 cars, beating the previous record set in 1965 of 1,090,863 vehicles. Sadly though, with Nordhoff's death the Beetle lost its last great champion – a direct line of descent from passionate creator Ferdinand Porsche to enthusiastic rescuer Ivan Hirst and his British colleagues and then from 1948 to the ex-Opel man. Although the Beetle was destined to survive for a further thirty-five years and indeed annual production figures, albeit briefly, exceeded

The Volkswagen
is a favourite in 136 countries.

Why?

those achieved by Nordhoff, Kurt Lotz – Volkswagen's new Director General in 1968 – quickly set the tone for the car's future. 'We had been immovable under a single director for twenty years', he

decreed. 'Now we had to move to a many faceted product.' As for the Beetle, Lotz's prophecy was that, 'Wolfsburg will never see the twenty-million mark … as we won't repeat Ford's mistake'.

production survey

INTRODUCTION

From January 1940, each Beetle chassis produced was duly numbered in series. Engines were also numbered from this point, as was the frame and body of each car. Frame numbers were discontinued in June 1955, while the practice of stamping each body came to an end exactly three years later in June 1958. Body numbers were zeroed in August 1955 – when the model year policy changed – and again at the end of June 1957.

The frame number was originally punched in by hand onto the flat area at the 'head' end of the chassis. From May 1945, the frame number was hand-punched into the frame tunnel – to the right-hand side – and beneath the rear seat.

The body number was punched into the metal below the petrol tank – the front body section – which formed a part of the spare wheel well.

A rectangular identification plate, made of brass and indicating the manufacturer, model, chassis number, engine number, vehicle weight and date of manufacture, was located immediately above the body number. With effect from 1950, a small plate, which read 'Made in Germany', was added below the body number. In October 1954 the identification plate became smaller and the year of manufacture was deleted. In 1955, the smaller plate was altered to read 'Made in Western Germany'. In January 1959, the small plate was discontinued.

Front axles were stamped with a number until the end of December 1964. After this date, until the end of July 1965, only axle numbers continued to be listed.

Engine numbers more or less remained the same in format until the arrival of the new 1300 model in August 1965. The deletion of the 30bhp engine, beloved of the Standard Model owner after the introduction of the more powerful 34bhp engine in August 1960 for the Deluxe, allowed a simple system to be adopted: 1200 engines were prefaced with the letters 'DO', while the 1300 engine had the designation 'FO'. The arrival of the 1500 engine a year later in August 1966 saw the adoption of the letters 'HO'.

Originally punched in by hand, after 13 October 1947 chassis numbers were punched in by stencil on the tunnel in a position between the gear lever and handbrake. Starting in 1959 chassis numbers (and other numbers) were grouped differently. The first numeral (2) was spaced from the other digits, creating two banks of three numbers, with a single numeral in front. For the 1965 model year (August 1964), a nine-digit chassis number was introduced. Key to an appreciation of these numbers was the third digit, which stood for the model year (for example, 115 000 001 – first number for the 1965 model year, starting August 1964).

In August 1955, Volkswagen adopted the American style of model year. Hence from 1 August 1955 to 31 July 1956, Volkswagen produced 1956 model year cars. Previously, the calendar year and model year were the same.

This early Beetle features a number plate pressing on the engine lid (pre-July 1949) and banana-shaped over-riders (pre May 1949). Other out of shot details help to confirm it to be of 1947 vintage.

1) TYPE AND MODEL DESIGNATIONS

In September 1945, one time plant manager under the British, Rudolph Brorman created a list of Beetle variants that could be manufactured. Based on the designs created by Ferdinand Porsche before and during the war years, a reasonable percentage of the types listed if built were not accurately recorded. In 1946, overall production increased dramatically, while after February all production was concentrated on the Type 11 – the 'saloon type, two-door'.

Type	Old type no.	Description	1945	1946 Jan–Sept
11	60	Saloon – two-door	58	7,677
13		Saloon – two-door with sliding roof		
15		Drop head coupé, two-door		
21	82	Kübelwagen	522	1
25		Fire tender with high-pressure water pump (K)		
27		Delivery van, open, with canopy (K)		
28		Delivery van, closed body (K)	219	
51	82E	Saloon – two-door with chassis 82 (Kübel chassis)	703	102
53		Saloon – two-door with chassis 82 & sliding roof		
55		Drop head coupé, two-door with sliding roof		
81		Delivery van, with canopy		
83		Delivery van, closed body – Reichspost type	275	
91		Trailer open		
93		Trailer closed	713	7
100		Road Tractor		

Cars produced after June 1949 and introduced before 1954 were designated as indicated in the table below.

Type number	Description
11A	Standard Saloon LHD
11B	Standard Saloon RHD
11C	Export/Deluxe Saloon LHD
11D	Export/Deluxe Saloon RHD
11E	Standard Sunroof Saloon LHD
11F	Standard Sunroof Saloon RHD
11G	Export/Deluxe Sunroof Saloon LHD
11H	Export/Deluxe Sunroof Saloon RHD
14A	Hebmüller 2+2 Cabriolet LHD
15A	Karmann Cabriolet LHD
15B	Karmann Cabriolet RHD
17	Miesen Ambulance on Type 11
18A	Police Cabriolet – Hebmüller, Papler, Austro Tatra & Karmann

Model designations were revised with effect from the beginning of 1954. The model designation changed on the ID plate from (for example) 1/11 to 11 in January 1959.

Type number	Description
1/11	Standard Saloon LHD
1/12	Standard Saloon RHD
1/13	Export/Deluxe LHD
1/14	Export/Deluxe RHD
1/15	Standard Sunroof Saloon LHD
1/16	Standard Sunroof Saloon RHD
1/17	Export/Deluxe Sunroof Saloon LHD
1/18	Export/Deluxe Sunroof Saloon RHD
1/41	Hebmüller 2+2 Cabriolet LHD (no longer in production)
1/51	Karmann Cabriolet LHD
1/52	Karmann Cabriolet RHD

For the 1964 model year, while the basic pattern of numbers remained, the model descriptions of necessity had been revised.

Type	Description
111	Saloon LHD with 30bhp engine
112	Saloon RHD with 30bhp engine
113	Deluxe Saloon LHD
114	Deluxe Saloon RHD
115	Saloon LHD with 30bhp engine and fabric fold-back sunroof
116	Saloon RHD with 30bhp engine and fabric fold-back sunroof
117	Deluxe Saloon LHD with steel wind-back sunroof
118	Deluxe Saloon RHD with steel wind-back sunroof
151	Karmann Cabriolet LHD
152	Karmann Cabriolet RHD

With the introduction of larger-engined Beetles, model designations became more complicated. The table below indicates the model designations in August 1967 – the first month of production after the period covered by this book, but incorporating the additional models introduced after the period covered by the previous table.

Type	Equipment extras	Description
111		VW 1200 LHD
112		VW 1200 RHD
115		VW 1200 LHD with steel wind-back sunroof
116		VW 1200 RHD with steel wind-back sunroof
113		VW 1300 LHD
114		VW 1300 RHD
117		VW 1300 LHD with steel wind-back sunroof
118		VW 1300 RHD with steel wind-back sunroof
113/4	M88	VW 1300 with 34bhp engine
113	M157 (44bhp engine)	VW 1500 LHD
114	M157 (44bhp engine)	VW 1500 RHD
151	M157 (44bhp engine)	Karmann Cabriolet LHD
152	M157 (44bhp engine)	Karmann Cabriolet RHD

Other Beetle-based models (not listed) included the Karmann Ghia Coupé and Cabriolet (141/142 and 143/144 respectively), plus the 147 – LHD only – delivery van often referred to as the Fridolin.

2) MONTHLY PRODUCTION DETAILS

All numbers refer to the last day of a given month, 1940–48 (summary – first and last numbers of each year).

Year	Month	Chassis number	Engine number
1940	January	00 001	00 001
1940	December	01 001	01 000
1941	January	01 001	01 101
1941	December	05 656	06 251
1942	January	05 657	06 252
1942	December	014 383	017 113
1943	January	014 348	017 114
1943	December	032 302	045 707
1944	January	032 303	045 708
1944	December	051 999	077 682
1945	January	052 000	077 683
1945	December	053 814	079 093
1946	January	053 815	079 094
1946	December	063 796	090 732
1947	January	063 797	090 733
1947	December	072 743	100 788
1948	January	073 853	N/A
1948	December	091 921	122 649

All years below represent the last unit for a given month unless otherwise indicated.

1949

Month	Chassis number	Engine number	Rear axle	Front axle	Frame number	Body number
January	94 461	125 337	104 549	102 973	100 282	44 376
February	97 061	128 157	107 150	105 558	103 132	47 096
March	100 236	131 440	110 853	108 853	106 628	50 111
April	102 888	134 135	113 415	111 619	109 040	52 764
May	106 438	137 650	116 903	115 107	112 780	56 279
June	110 248	141 520	120 680	118 997	116 748	60 161
July	114 530	145 750	124 910	123 207	121 176	64 379
August	119 196	150 342	129 410	128 706	125 920	69 134
September	123 876	154 934	133 875	132 307	130 890	73 743
October	128 754	159 789	138 705	137 298	135 940	78 446
November	133 615	164 739	143 665	142 239	140 880	83 175
December	138 554	169 913	148 658	147 131	145 893	87 959

1950

Month	Chassis number	Engine number	Rear axle	Front axle	Frame number	Body number
January	144 319	176 082	154 644	152 939	151 870	93 558
February	149 883	182 051	160 805	158 549	157 640	98 979
March	156 683	189 501	168 255	165 431	164 676	105 604
April	162 448	196 053	174 872	171 274	170 759	111 331
May	169 063	203 321	182 142	178 027	177 537	117 821
June	176 987	212 397	191 321	185 952	185 471	125 425
July	182 236	217 562	196 183	190 254	190 195	129 573
August	189 755	227 925	206 939	198 831	199 070	137 901
September	197 739	237 607	216 847	206 666	207 075	145 182
October	205 956	247 840	226 969	215 193	215 710	153 826
November	213 957	257 816	237 027	223 346	223 774	161 755
December	220 133	265 600	244 739	229 566	230 200	167 642

1951

Month	Chassis number	Engine number	Rear axle	Front axle	Frame number	Body number
January	228 324	275 851	255 108	238 967	238 850	175 714
February	235 856	285 206	264 612	245 647	246 862	183 956
March	242 698	293 651	273 219	252 962	253 993	189 266
April	248 875	301 201	280 810	259 363	260 351	195 466
May	255 651	309 400	289 154	266 138	267 800	202 053
June	263 981	319 600	299 023	274 595	276 500	210 021
July	272 486	330 000	308 917	283 266	285 550	217 993
August	281 220	340 200	318 894	292 321	294 500	226 288
September	289 399	350 250	328 624	301 146	303 100	234 027
October	298 569	361 200	339 430	311 036	312 250	242 883
November	307 652	371 950	350 045	320 435	321 650	251 527
December	313 829	379 470	357 435	326 619	328 800	257 467

1952

The introduction of a synchromesh gearbox (2nd, 3rd, and 4th) for the Export model in October 1952 resulted in two rear axle listings – A with synchromesh – numbers only, crash box as before. (From 1956, rear axle crash shown in a separate column.)

Month	Chassis number	Engine number	Rear axle	Front axle	Frame number	Body number
January	322 798	390 123	367 597	335 839	337 237	266 047
February	331 318	400 481	377 391	344 487	345 926	274 279
March	339 822	410 904	387 556	352 985	354 787	282 481
April	348 714	422 195	398 361	361 888	363 949	291 011
May	358 632	434 255	410 421	371 855	374 492	300 383
June	368 640	446 267	422 475	382 830	385 835	310 006
July	375 154	454 005	430 280	388 326	391 693	315 999
August	385 990	466 885	443 360	399 227	403 360	326 343
September	397 014	480 355	456 613	410 428	414 700	337 454
October	408 537	494 569	A – 8 324 461 735	421 868	426 563	348 672
November	418 301	506 974	A – 16 312 465 916	431 888	436 746	358 168
December	428 156	519 136	A – 24 736 469 555	442 001	466 790	367 730

1953

Month	Chassis number	Engine number	Rear axle	Front axle	Frame number	Body number
January	440 292	533 991	A – 35 618 473 255	454 251	459 523	379 360
February	451 312	547 210	A – 46 545 476 655	465 331	470 762	389 824
March	464 207	562 963	A – 58 543 479 410	478 386	484 730	402 089
April	476 152	577 544	A – 71 124 481 517	490 536	497 199	413 308
May	487 413	591 102	A – 82 698 483 657	501 936	508 687	423 929
June	501 382	607 846	A – 97 074 486 220	516 011	522 707	437 068
July	509 668	617 552	A – 105 256 487 730	524 217	531 133	444 789
August	522 314	632 573	A – 117 815 490 180	536 923	544 291	456 886
September	536 873	650 018	A – 132 271 493 072	551 411	559 147	471 191
October	551 743	667 834	A – 146 828 496 219	566 418	575 067	486 096
November	565 499	683 907	A – 159 344 499 974	580 165	589 202	499 625
December	579 682	700 697	A – 172 034 503 903	594 416	604 242	513 563

1954

Month	Chassis number	Engine number	Rear axle	Front axle	Frame number	Body number
January	594 689	718 594	A – 186 768 506 934	609 486	619 094	527 627
February	609 909	737 005	A – 202 724 509 500	624 666	635 031	514 891
March	627 474	758 796	A – 221 180 512 398	642 265	653 185	558 718
April	643 364	778 134	A – 237 604 515 143	658 300	669 226	573 917
May	660 135	798 378	A – 255 147 517 961	675 135	685 583	588 783
June	676 878	818 785	A – 272 627 520 782	691 945	702 589	604 731
July	687 170	831 283	A – 238 331 522 440	702 239	713 366	614 378
August	703 464	850 932	A – 300 458 525 127	718 544	730 645	629 679
September	722 716	870 071	A – 319 985 528 571	737 728	749 938	648 061
October	742 329	897 572	A – 339 982 532 178	757 434	768 021	666 144
November	761 706	921 247	A – 360 083 535 440	777 234	788 347	683 979
December	781 884	945 526	A – 380 323 538 982	797 194	809 236	702 231

1955

Body numbers were zeroed in August for the new format 1956 model year. From early June 1955 frame numbers were withdrawn.

Month	Chassis number	Engine number	Rear axle	Front axle	Frame number	Body number
January	802 662	970 181	A – 401 939 542 325	819 069	830 297	721 033
February	823 664	994 884	A – 423 919 545 093	839 069	851 138	739 709
March	847 966	1023 849	A – 449 934 548 039	863 603	876 669	761 863
April	869 399	1049 452	A – 472 886 550 700	885 374	899 040	781 224
May	892 300	1076 697	A – 497 247 553 394	908 334	922 102	802 297
June	916 456	1105 932	A – 523 384 556 411	932 819		824 564
July	929 512	1121 833	A – 537 429 558 296	946 104		to 828 328 from 000 001 to 008 056
August	953 486	1150 857	A – 563 052 561 588	970 643		030 789
September	981 573	1182 658	A – 591 442 564 870	997 608		055 712
October	1008 157	1213 907	A – 619 979 567 848	1024 218		079 843
November	1034 731	1245 382	A – 648 768 570 531	1050 973		104 231
December	1060 929	1277 347	A – 677 497 573 609	1078 268		128 500

1956

Month	Chassis number	Engine number	Rear axle	Rear axle crash	Front axle	Body number
January	1089 519	1311 073	A – 708 286	576 517	1107 103	154 046
February	1117 569	1344 312	A – 738 626	579 208	1135 298	179 277
March	1146 396	1377 738	A – 769 872	581 490	1163 988	204 286
April	1173 573	1410 503	A – 799 835	583 864	1191 770	228 314
May	1201 428	1443 582	A – 830 284	586 080	1219 444	252 873
June	1231 530	1479 028	A – 862 838	588 573	1249 297	279 212
July	1246 318	1495 945	A – 878 094	598 981	1263 499	291 543
August	1276 742	1533 485	A – 911 910	601 849	1294 274	318 845
September	1305 700	1569 111	A – 944 076	604 789	1323 273	344 124
October	1338 159	1609 290	A – 981 094	608 073	1356 043	373 163
November	1368 326	1646 240	A1014 730	611 195	1386 153	399 924
December	1394 119	1678 209	A1044 024	613 554	1411 994	423 122

1957

Body numbers were zeroed at the end of June 1957.

Month	Chassis number	Engine number	Rear axle	Rear axle crash	Front axle	Body number
January	1427 291	1719 310	A1082 258	616 471	1445 224	453 507
February	1457 750	1756 879	A1114 506	618 852	1475 669	481 329
March	1490 537	1797 568	A1152 596	621 186	1508 504	510 823
April	1521 755	1836 437	A1189 006	623 124	1539 885	538 206
May	1555 242	1878 857	A1228 629	625 231	1573 589	567 604
June	1584 654	1916 070	A1262 974	627 617	1603 202	to 583 692 from 000 001 to 009 560
July	1600 846	1937 052	A1282 034	629 151	1619 741	23 794
August	1637 038	1982 625	A1324 871	631 796	1655 694	56 005
September	1671 208	2026 514	A1365 885	634 121	1689 918	86 044
October	1709 420	2074 250	A1410 500	636 656	1727 791	119 419
November	1742 856	2116 308	A1450 322	638 807	1761 186	148 538
December	1774 680	2156 321	A1488 444	640 822	1794 383	176 061

1958

Body numbers were withdrawn on the last day of June 1958.

Month	Chassis number	Engine number	Rear axle	Rear axle crash	Front axle	Body number
January	1815 645	2206 943	A1537 488	643 226	1836 295	211 863
February	1852 703	2252 831	A1581 612	645 097	1873 729	243 798
March	1891 481	2300 862	A1627 634	646 903	1912 412	277 213
April	1926 948	2345 671	A1670 346	648 762	1948 858	307 949
May	1962 835	2390 818	A1712 759	650 521	1984 628	338 686
June	2001 110	2439 544	A1759 027	652 071	2023 359	364 474
July	2020 302	2463 618	A1781 921	652 901	2042 172	
August	2060 332	2514 115	A1829 393	655 358	2082 535	
September	2102 988	2567 730	A1880 455	657 658	2125 241	
October	2149 028	2624 613	A1934 870	660 208	2170 759	
November	2186 987	2671 821	A1979 731	662 472	2208 760	
December	2226 206	2721 313	A2027 204	664 479	2248 750	

1959

Revision to numbering system – spacing the first numeral from the rest.

Month	Chassis number	Engine number	Rear axle	Rear axle crash	Front axle
January	2 270 326	2 775 897	A 2 079 110	666 409	2 292 842
February	2 312 649	2 828 764	A 2 129 671	668 199	2 335 643
March	2 355 192	2 881 524	A 2 180 087	669 946	2 378 729
April	2 405 422	2 943 920	A(B) 2 240 909	671 767	2 429 561
May	2 447 564	2 996 628	A(B) 2 291 032	673 400	2 471 793
June	2 498 431	3 059 836	A(B) 2 351 334	675 363	2 522 173
July	2 528 282	3 098 191	A(B) 2 387 664	676 657	2 552 345
August	2 574 497	3 152 785	A(B) 2 442 042	678 107	2 597 062
September	2 631 447	3 218 812	A(B) 2 511 059	680 201	2 653 399
October	2 690 897	3 288 594	A(B) 2 583 015	682 177	2 710 961
November	2 745 953	3 355 542	A(B) 2 647 593	684 021	2 764 721
December	2 801 613	3 424 453	A(B) 2 712 903	685 788	2 819 706

1960

From the start of the 1961 model year it is necessary to distinguish between the 34bhp engine of the Deluxe model and the old 30bhp engine still allocated to the Standard.

Month	Chassis number	Engine number	Engine no. 30bhp	Rear axle	Rear axle crash	Front axle
January	2 862 052	3 598 973		A(B) 2 780 435	687 705	2 874 732
February	2 922 174	3 658 782		A(B) 2 851 293	689 467	2 933 392
March	2 988 365	3 726 116		A(B) 2 931 154	691 256	3 000 092
April	3 048 367	3 786 158		A(B) 3 005 555	693 122	3 058 094
May	3 115 196	3 852 394		A(B) 3 086 252	695 089	3 122 843
June	3 178 360	3 909 830		A(B) 3 160 330	697 015	3 184 697
July	3 204 566	3 927 802		A(B) 3 175 096	697 382	3 203 961
August	3 267 185	5 073 407	3 900 380	A(B) 3 244 458	699 178	3 273 061
September	3 335 847	5 157 563	3 902 552	A(B) 3 326 526	700 679	3 339 738
October	3 405 533	5 223 966	3 903 778	A(B) 3 468 638	701 544	3 405 251
November	3 478 068	5 307 207	3 905 430	A(B) 3 551 583	702 399	3 474 449
December	3 551 044	5 428 637	3 907 587	A(B) 3 637 181	703 268	3 543 878

1961

Month	Chassis number	Engine number	Engine no. 30bhp	Rear axle	Rear axle crash	Front axle
January	3 628 283	5 519 478	3 908 278	A(B)3 728 422	704 331	3 617 800
February	3 701 251	5 601 896	3 909 491	A(B)3 789 075	705 497	3 685 841
March	3 780 308	5 689 700	3 915 041	A(B)3 875 275	706 702	3 758 320
April	3 860 285	5 766 200	3 920 073	A(B)3 952 606	707 843	3 822 437
May	3 919 200	5 849 650	3 921 898	A(B)4 044 033	709 158	3 892 189
June	4 000 004	5 938 194	3 923 766	A(B)4 121 534	710 899	3 966 265
July	4 020 589	5 958 948	3 924 023	A(B)4 143 539	711 008	3 985 791
August	4 090 311	6 045 560	3 925 592	A(B)4 231 694	712 468	4 060 539
September	4 165 011	6 128 600	3 927 056	A(B)4 314 391	713 895	4 132 150
October	4 245 397	6 219 138	3 928 695	A(B)4 402 163	715 373	4 206 737
November	4 321 188	6 309 500	3 930 100	A(B)4 486 331	716 716	4 277 378
December	4 400 051	6 375 945	3 931 468	A(B)4 458 031	718 205	4 340 919

1962

Month	Chassis number	Engine number	Engine no. 30bhp	Rear axle	Rear axle crash	Front axle
January	4 464 262	6 463 435	3 933 796	A(B)4 533 831	720 200	4 416 685
February	4 534 234	6 547 999	3 935 615	A(B)4 619 400	721 630	4 490 677
March	4 609 564	6 642 050	3 937 702	A(B)4 714 961	723 091	4 569 912
April	4 681 428	6 726 000	3 938 753	A(B)4 794 252	724 563	4 636 239
May	4 790 219	6 819 440	3 940 642	A(B)4 884 024	726 286	4 714 753
June	4 835 210	6 904 001	3 942 538	A(B)4 970 873	728 327	4 787 324
July	4 854 999	6 935 203	3 942 914	A(B)4 998 786	728 398	4 812 009
August	4 932 385	7 032 385	3 944 599	A(B)5 096 312	729 981	4 893 693
September	5 007 072	7 116 931	3 946 175	A(B)5 182 010	731 507	4 967 159
October	5 092 087	7 215 250	3 948 020	A(B)5 280 165	733 229	5 049 425
November	5 168 250	7 313 000	3 949 107	A(B)5 372 286	734 369	5 128 209
December	5 225 042	7 373 000	3 949 823	A(B)5 438 170	734 678	5 184 288

1963

Month	Chassis number	Engine number	Engine no. 30bhp	Rear axle	Rear axle crash	Front axle
January	5 288 727	7 451 023	3 950 852	A(B)5 514 032	735 995	5 250 367
February	5 342 227	7 517 180	3 952 532	A(B)5 582 005	737 320	5 300 750
March	5 419 800	7 605 922	3 954 241	A(B)5 677 044	738 940	5 380 837
April	5 497 061	7 687 919	3 955 722	A(B)5 766 157	740 413	5 456 672
May	5 578 121	7 777 337	3 957 472	A(B)5 863 073	742 142	5 537 602
June	5 643 229	7 852 564	3 958 756	A(B)5 941 424	743 457	5 603 141
July	5 677 118	7 893 118	3 959 303	A(B)5 983 874	744 058	5 639 728
August	5 750 180	7 972 456	3 960 976	A(B)6 051 093	744 876	5 709 237
September	5 815 300	8 047 902	3 961 624	A(B)6 132 442	746 260	5 777 220
October	5 889 417	8 130 544	3 963 059	A(B)6 222 135	747 483	5 850 544
November	5 961 053	8 207 484	3 964 389	A(B)6 307 987	748 724	5 921 375
December	6 016 120	8 264 628	3 965 218	A(B)6 374 977	749 642	5 974 780

1964

From August 1964 a nine-digit chassis number replaced the previous numbering system, with the third digit representing the model year. Front axle numbers were no longer stamped after December 1964, while the gearbox A(B) prefix was no longer listed after October 1964. The crash box was discontinued at the end of October 1964. The apparent reverse in 30bhp engine numbers in June 1964 is correct, as one series of numbers had been passed over in May of the same year.

Month	Chassis number	Engine number	Engine no. 30bhp	Rear axle	Rear axle crash	Front axle
January	6 092 060	8 348 273	3 966 304	A(B)6 467 371	750 759	6 051 971
February	6 182 046	8 431 660	3 967 258	A(B)6 559 649	751 817	6 126 716
March	6 240 170	8 511 320	3 968 415	A(B)6 650 281	752 969	6 201 315
April	6 321 709	8 605 206	3 969 987	A(B)6 750 579	758 739	6 282 786
May	6 391 125	8 679 000	3 974 958	A(B)6 832 479	759 859	6 351 371
June	6 479 490	8 765 492	3 972 001	A(B)6 928 673	761 911	6 432 004
July	6 502 399	8 796 622	3 972 440	A(B)6 963 436	762 505	6 461 156
August	115 073 129	8 887 988	3 973 458	A(B)7 051 272	763 235	6 535 269
September	115 161 387	8 968 669	3 975 990	A(B)7 156 437	764 596	6 621 924
October	115 252 151	9 057 000	3 976 971	A(B)7 262 094	765 263	6 715 916
November	115 331 160	9 129 760	3 981 431	7 361 634		6 799 388
December	115 410 000	9 339 890	3 984 729	7 454 229		6 873 511

1965

In January 1965 the Standard model was replaced by the 1200A. Initially still allocated a 30bhp engine, the 1200A benefited from the synchromesh gearbox. The apparent error relating to 30bhp engine numbers in June and July 1965 in reality refers to free numbers from January 1960!

Month	Chassis number	Engine number	Engine no. 1200A	Rear axle	Front axle
January	115 500 000	9 389 000	3 989 871	7 552 095	6 957 154
February	115 574 322	9 284 780	3 994 992	7 653 509	7 044 273
March	115 678 203	9 371 458	4 002 980	7 769 967	7 145 359
April	115 767 035	9 552 548	4 010 965	7 875 264	7 236 786
May	115 861 006	9 635 887	4 018 015	7 983 793	7 329 550
June	115 967 150	9 724 765	3 539 951	8 093 038	7 422 827
July	115 979 202	9 725 086	3 546 988	8 131 843	7 455 788

1965–66

With the arrival of the new 1300 Beetle and the deletion of the 30bhp engine from the range a new engine numbering system was devised. 1200 engine numbers were prefixed with the letters DO and the 1300 with FO. Front axle numbers were no longer listed with effect from 1 August 1965.

Month	Chassis number	Engine no. 1200	Engine no. 1300
August	116 102 780	DO 016 999	FO 115 030
September	116 204 348	DO 025 804	FO 200 258
October	116 302 145	DO 039 099	FO 288 690
November	116 382 728	DO 046 362	FO 362 495
December	116 463 103	DO 050 314	FO 442 242
January	116 543 112	DO 053 049	FO 521 075
February	116 622 320	DO 060 706	FO 594 000
March	116 723 045	DO 071 814	FO 684 880
April	116 809 563	DO 080 210	FO 763 341
May	116 909 207	DO 088 453	FO 850 026
June	116 1017 006	DO 095 000	FO 940 716
July	116 1021 298	DO 095 049	

1966–67

Month	Chassis number	Engine no. 1200	Engine no. 1300	Engine no. 1500
August	117 109 832	DO 106 475	FO 955 582	HO 350 785
September	117 202 292	DO 112 299	FO 977 027	HO 411 076
October	117 288 898	DO 144 244	FI 020 000	HO 470 199
November	117 363 979	DO 118 984	FI 038 224	HO 528 818
December	117 422 503	DO 120 750	FI 057 754	HO 576 613
January	117 505 826	DO 131 796	FI 073 754	HO 621 556
February	117 566 719	DO 149 103	FI 088 186	HO 647 064
March	117 620 975	DO 166 874	FI 103 452	HO 661 348
April	117 674 558	DO 184 053	FI 126 528	HO 679 371
May	117 739 188	DO 204 920	FI 153 002	HO 802 478
June	117 817 896	DO 222 992	FI 167 322	HO 840 170
July	117 844 902	DO 324 014	FI 237 506	HO 874 199

3) PRODUCTION NUMBERS

Between 1940 and 1944 some 630 KdF-Wagens were produced and between 1943 and 1945 a further 688 Type 82E vehicles – the saloon with Kübel chassis – might be added to the production total.

The chart below indicates total Beetle production by year, with comparative figures for other selected models, as well as total production figures for Volkswagen AG and the Volkswagen Group. There was a European-wide recession in 1967. Figures for 1968 saw the Beetle bounce back to a figure exceeding its previous best year of 1965.

Year	Beetle	Transporter	VW 1500	Volkswagen GMBH/AG	Volkswagen Group
1945	1,785			1,785	
1946	10,020			10,020	
1947	8,987			8,987	
1948	19,244			19,244	
1949	46,154			46,154	
1950	81,979	8,059		90,038	
1951	93,709	12,003		105,712	
1952	114,348	21,665		136,013	
1953	151,323	28,417		179,740	
1954	202,174	40,199		242,373	
1955	279,986	49,907		329,893	
1956	333,190	62,500		395,690	
1957	380,561	91,993		472,554	
1958	451,526	105,562		553,399	557,088
1959	575,407	129,836		696,860	705,243
1960	739,455	151,218		865,858	890,673
1961	827,850	168,600	10,663	959,773	1,007,113
1962	877,014	180,377	127,324	1,112,424	1,184,675
1963	838,488	189,294	181,809	1,132,080	1,209,591
1964	948,370	200,325	262,020	1,317,295	1,410,715
1965	1,090,863	189,876	261,915	1,447,660	1,594,861
1966	1,080,165	191,373	311,701	1,476,509	1,650,487
1967	925,787	162,741	201,800	1,162,258	1,339,823

4) NOTABLE PRODUCTION DATES

14 October 1946	10,000th Beetle
4 March 1950	100,000th Beetle
5 October 1951	250,000th Beetle
10 March 1953	Change from split to oval rear window
5 July 1953	500,000th Beetle
5 August 1955	1,000,000th Beetle
1 August 1957	Production of revised model with much larger rear window and new dashboard begins
28 December 1957	2,000,000th Beetle
25 August 1959	3,000,000th Beetle
15 June 1960	500,000th Beetle exported to the USA
9 November 1960	4,000,000th Beetle
5 December 1961	5,000,000th Beetle
15 September 1965	10,000,000th Beetle
1965	Beetle production exceeds one million cars in a twelve-month period for the first time (1,090,863 cars worldwide)
1 August 1967	Substantially revised Beetle with vertically set headlamps, shortened boot and engine lids, box-section bumpers, etc. introduced

Suspension

All four wheels of the Volkswagen are individually suspended, and each has its independent torsion bar.
In front, two parallel connected transverse tubes each enclose a full-length square torsion bar consisting of eight spring leaves; each is attached to the appropriate trailing arm. These trailing arms form parallelograms which give ideal spring geometry and progressively increasing spring power, no matter what the driving conditions. Bumps actuating the springs do not alter the wheel track. The rear axle consists of two swing axle shafts, whose springing is likewise mutually independent. A full-length transverse tube encloses two torsion bars supported at the centre of the frame; these, connected by spring braces with the axle shafts, give each wheel individual springing. This torsion-bar springing, carefully balanced in itself and progressively snubbed by long-stroke hydraulic, telescopic shock absorbers, keeps the car from nodding or bouncing.

The smooth underbody of the Volkswagen offers the least possible wind resistance. It is stamped of high-grade sheet steel, and down its longitudinal axis is an electrically welded centre beam that forks at the rear to receive the engine and gearbox assembly. Body and underbody, joined and rubber sealed, form a single torsion-resistant unit.

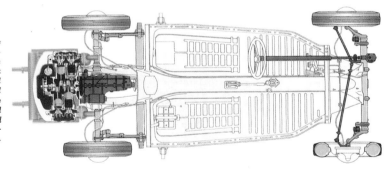

5 specification detail changes
month by month

The following survey endeavours to summarize all the important detail specification changes made to the Beetle over the period 1949 – and the introduction of the Export or Deluxe model – to July 1967 and the end of the period covered by this volume. However, the changes referred to are in no way intended to be restricted to just the Export model. Equally important is the often forgotten Standard model – later the 1200A, while some of the changes affecting the Karmann Cabriolet are also listed.

Although it might have been of benefit to list to the same level of detail Beetles built before the Export model watershed, the practicalities of reporting all the somewhat ad-hoc, car-to-car variations and spec additions would have resulted in an inevitably suspect or incomplete document. A general description of the Beetle is given.

The changes listed are only pertinent in their entirety to Beetles produced at the Wolfsburg factory, or in later years at the other German satellite factories. For example, the variances detectable in Brazilian-built Beetles, or CKD (completely knocked down) kits assembled in Australia, either relate to a different pattern of evolution in the case of the former, or the use of a percentage of locally sourced materials in the latter instance. Conversely, changes made to the specification of Beetles built in Germany for export to, for example, the United States are listed, as these cars were still entirely manufactured at Wolfsburg or a German satellite and merely shipped to the destination market.

As referred to in the previous chapter, Volkswagen's policy regarding calendar years changed in August 1955, when the American style of break in a twelve-month period was adopted. In an attempt to simplify the arrangement to a reader's eye, each post-August 1955 year is highlighted – for example '1959 model year' would refer to manufacture between August 1958 and July 1959. Calendar years are retained, however, in an attempt to cover all angles of the Beetle's evolution.

PRE-EXPORT MODEL BEETLES

Pre-export model Beetles portrayed a range of characteristics, as noted below.

- All-steel body bolted to lightweight platform chassis with central backbone and seal between the two (see below).
- Bodyshell made from a number of panels welded together including: roof; front and rear valance; front and rear cross-member (both of which are bolted to and sit on the floorpan); rear luggage compartment; front luggage compartment floor; floor and back of well for spare wheel; two rear quarter panels (including window cut-outs), inner wings front and rear (the former joined by the front valance); sills (designed to facilitate the movement of warm air from exhaust heater boxes to the interior of the car, via footwell outlets at

both sides of the car); a large panel forming the dashboard; the lower 'A' posts and the inner sections of the windscreen pillars.
- Evidence that some roof panels in immediate post-war period made out of three sections lap-welded together due to shortages.
- At the front of the Beetle – curved bonnet, strengthened by convex centre strip and embossed edges in pressing process. Boot fastened with simple but locking handle (facing upwards) and similar in nature to that used for the engine compartment lid. Boot lid hinged internally and held open with basic collapsing/sliding strut. Convex roof pressing centrally located above the windscreen – intended for securing windscreen-mounted aerial for accessory radio. Large horn mounted on bracket behind and above left front wing (normally Bosch). Headlamp trim rings finished in painted metal, as were plain bumpers (moulded rubber grommets fitted around the bumper brackets). Headlamp lenses usually marked with VW insignia, but made by Hella, or Bosch (some war shortage and early post-war Beetles fitted with Kübelwagen headlamps – that is, vertical lenses).
- Wartime KdF-Wagens fitted with cylindrical petrol tank supported by brackets concealed by metal panels. Triangular panel in front designed as mounting for spare wheel. Replaced in 1945 by 8gal (36ltr) rectangular tank with large 100mm diameter fuel cap.
- At the rear of the Beetle – two small rear windows with central vertical division over forty-two vertical louvres designed to allow the engine's fan to suck in cooling air. Sculptured 'W'-shaped engine lid with pressing for registration plate and prominent VW embossed housing for stop light; nicknamed 'Pope's nose'. Engine lid hinged internally at top. Simple vertically positioned handle to open engine compartment lid. Aperture beneath engine compartment lid for starting handle with locating guide fixed to rear bumper. Small wing-mounted tail lights – left- and right-hand pairs to accommodate the curvature of

the wings (aluminium bezel around the glass lens). Exhaust tailpipe position varied, as mainly built by hand. Some KdF-Wagens had a centrally mounted tailpipe – most common position; certainly post-war – below right-hand end of rear valance.
- The Beetle's wings bolted to the remainder of the bodywork. Exposed front hinges on doors. Pull-out handles for both doors – only driver's side lockable. Plate-glass door windows lacked quarter lights (no inlaid bright trim around any of the windows). Grooved, matching pair, dark yellow/orange-coloured semaphore indicators – solenoid operated, electro-mechanical; located in the 'B' posts. Metal running boards fitted under doors and rear quarter-panels, usually covered (ribbed rubber, without any additional trim). Hubcaps stamped with VW emblem – slightly revised in 1945 (disappearance of inner annular groove), but all with prominent nipple design until late 1947.
- The post-war Beetle's interior was particularly spartan. Allegedly, some cars lacked seat covers of any nature, while others were issued minus a woollen headlining (military personnel may have sat on their stores-provided coats in such circumstances). The tubular-framed seats were normally padded with horsehair and covered in harsh woolcloth. The interior panels were made from stiff cardboard, covered in either woolcloth, or possibly the more expensive/scarce leatherette. Fore and aft adjustment of the seats was only possible by unscrewing large wing nuts on top of the rails. The woollen headliner, where fitted, only extended to the roof panel. (reveals embossed metal below rear windows – intended to add strength to body). Door furniture was painted (ten and a half turns to lower the window; door locked by pushing handle to 'detent' position). Rubber mats on floor of the majority of cars, but dependent on availability. Most KdF-Wagens lacked an interior light, although by 1945 a circular light above and between the two rear windows was the norm. Rear luggage

compartment sometimes fitted with wooden rails to cater for heavier items.

- Most Beetles had a three-spoke, narrow-rim steering wheel finished in black – although some wartime cars had thick spokes as per the Kübelwagen. The push-horn button was located at the wheel's centre. Simple metal dash comprised of open, all-metal 'pockets' at either end, plus a black-faced speedometer to the left-centre and body-coloured metal blanking panel embossed with VW insignia to the right centre. A knob above and between these two features of early Beetles operated the semaphore indicators. The speedometer – with white characters and calibrated to 120km/h – was designed to appear to be operating backwards, but in reality was entirely conventional. A VW emblem was prominent at the top of the dial. Recommended gear-change points were marked on the speedometer at 20, 40 and 62.5km/h respectively. Switches to the left and right of the speedometer, but still contained within the panel, operated the wipers and lights respectively. Between the two and at the base of the panel was the ignition switch, while a separate starter button was found at the bottom of the dash. Single plastic sun visor for driver.
- All Beetles lacked a petrol gauge, instead relying on a reserve fuel lever, which was positioned above the passenger footwell on the forward panel (vertical when not in use – turn to the right, clockwise to release the reserve gallon). A headlamp dipswitch was located above the driver's footwell to the left of the clutch pedal. The brake, clutch and accelerator cluster were attached to a base tube, which also formed an appropriate chassis mounting. The brake and clutch pedals were capped with rectangular ribbed rubbers bearing the VW symbol. The accelerator lacked a conventional treadle arrangement, instead relying on a small roller pedal (cables for the clutch and accelerator were tucked away in the Beetle's central backbone). Slightly forwards and to

the right of the straight gearlever – sometimes with an embossed VW insignia on the black knob – was a black choke-button marked with the letter 'L' for *luftklapper* – literally 'air-flapper valve'. The choke cable also ran through the Beetle's backbone.

- Beetles were fitted with five stud-pressed steel wheels, shod initially with 4.50 × 16 tube type tyres, but these soon gave way to 5.00 × 16 ones, invariably produced by Continental. All tyres were of a cross-ply nature.
- From the start, Beetles had a 6V electrical system. The battery was located under the rear seat on the right-hand-side of the floorpan. To reiterate, the rear wing-mounted reflectors supported by one bulb behind each sufficed as tail lights, while the single stop light was located within the 'Pope's nose' number-plate light cover. The windscreen wipers were driven through a linkage from a small Bosch electric motor (shortages during the period 1945–47 resulted in a number of cars being sent out with a single blade fitted at the driver's side). A Bosch starter motor was supplemented by a rarely required starting handle (*see* above).
- The gearbox was bolted to the rear end of the chassis pan and to the engine. Split both vertically and longitudinally, the ribbed alloy-cased unit lacked any form of synchronization. The rolling chassis consisted of two ribbed floorpans welded to a central tunnel and at the rear forming a fork to which the gearbox was mounted. Independent suspension by means of transversely mounted torsion bars contained in two cylindrical tubes at both the front and rear of the vehicle. Upper and lower parallel trailing arms, with damping by lever-type single-acting shock absorbers. Drive from the gearbox to the rear wheels through swinging half-axles, again running in cylindrical tubes. 1945 jacking points round – if fitted at all – but conventional and much safer square-box section points standard from 1946. Steering by transverse link and unequal length track rods –

worm and nut steering box fixed to upper front torsion bar tube.

- Cable-operated drum brakes on all four wheels. Four cables each operated under tension and enclosed in protective tube. Handbrake cable attached to a ratchet to the handbrake linkage rod, which ran through the central backbone/tunnel and operated on all four wheels. Front drums 230.1mm diameter – rear 230mm. Shoes front and rear 30mm in width.

1946

- Pushrod tubes with compressible corrugated tube ends, certain cars only (chassis number 054 617).
- Fuel tank fitted higher (chassis number 057 722).
- Noise reduction in engine compartment with fitting of sound-deadening cardboard (chassis number 057 893).
- Brake cable with lubrication nipple (chassis number 059 107).
- Tyres 5.00 × 16 (chassis number 059 107).

1947

- Rear hubs – reinforced ball bearings (chassis number 064 340).
- Spare wheel secured by chain with lock in well (chassis number 071 377).
- Fan housing fitted with manually adjustable flap closing half of air-intake aperture – summer and winter setting (chassis number 071 616).
- Chassis number punched in by stencil on chassis tunnel between gear lever and handbrake (chassis number 073 348, 13/10/47).

1948

- Crankshaft – 48.5mm diameter for flywheel. Flywheel 48.5mm bore (chassis number 076 722, 04/48).
- Unsprung choke cable (chassis number 073 816).
- Steering column – longitudinal groove for steering lock (chassis number 090 690).
- Modifications to brake drums – oil deflector and spacer widths increased to 15.9–16.1mm (chassis number 090 784).

specification detail changes month by month

1949

- Export/Deluxe production started on 2 June 1949 – chassis number 10 106 636.
- First production Karmann Cabriolet, 6 June; chassis dates to March 1949, 10 099 906 – semaphores originally in front quarter panel; by late 1949 relocated to position behind doors on rear quarter panel.

Date	Chassis no.	Change
Jan	091914	Double heating conduit – single to double heater cable
Jan	092918	Mushroom-shaped air filter
Jan	092879	Petrol stopcock – Thiokol seal
Jan	093270	Warm air channel lower part – heat flap without hinge
Jan	093781	Backrest straight on front seats (formerly leaning)
Jan	093834	Accelerator cable – elbow replaces eye
Feb	094554	Inlet manifold bracket/support
Feb	094470	Rear luggage compartment – two lengthwise rails added
Mar	096978	Control discontinued on air-cooling fan
Mar	098400	Gearbox oil 2.5ltr (previously 3.0ltr)
Apr	100826	Fuel pump with blue Solex diaphragm fitted with four gaskets
Apr	101322	Torsion bars – lower five-leaf, upper four-leaf (reverses previous pattern)
Apr	102026	Gearboxes now standard in Electron
Apr	101902	Case-hardened stems on exhaust valves
Apr	102537	Extra lubrication nipple on alloy pedal bearing
May	1-0102948	Bakelite blanking panel inset on dash (for radio)
		Bowden cable opens boot
		Engine lid no longer lockable. Bumpers – wider section
		Banana-style convex overriders discontinued – new overriders more rounded and smaller design
May	1-0102383	*EXPORT MODEL*
		Three-spoke steering wheel finished in ivory colour, or new two-spoke steering wheel again in ivory; both had plain horn button – larger on the two-spoke version and with aluminium surround; the three-spoke version had been phased out by the end of 1949
		Control knobs also ivory – glove compartments and instrument panel surrounds, chrome trim added
		Ivory trim extended to door furniture and gear-lever knob
May	1-0102848	Fuse box repositioned – now on left front side panel
May	1-0103039	Heater cable – channels end with rubber stoppers
May	1-0103168	Fibre material secured with strap replaces all-metal glove compartment arrangement
May		Brake light bulb – 6V, 15W
Jun		*EXPORT MODEL*
		Chrome finished bumpers, hubcaps, headlamp rims, door handles
		Interior fittings better quality – bolsters added to rear seats
		Solid cast aluminium, touching 'V' over 'W', symbol top centre of boot panel
		Horn repositioned behind left wing – previously mounted on left front bumper bracket; round horn grille on wing in front of horn, cut-out in wing – dummy grille to match on other side, no cut-out in wing – grilles stamped brass or aluminium and finished either in black or polished (from 1950 grilles standardized as polished aluminium)
		Rear light casing changed, necessitating removal of whole assembly from wing to change bulb (previously hold and pull outside of lens/trim ring – secured by small metal spring clips); bright metal trim ring (dropped in 1950)
Jun		Rear-view mirror secured, stopping vibration
Jun	1-0106637	Breather pipe
Jun	1-0106717	Anti-condensation protection in reflectors at rear of car
Jun	1-0108091	Filter in ventilation holes of cylinder head
Jul	1-0111054	Pressing for number plate on engine lid deleted
Jul	1-0114186	Felt cone air filter for engine (Export model)
Aug	1-0116375	Modified fuel tank shape – no gauze strainer and central tap; size increased and cap, still 100mm, now bore VW insignia

Date	Chassis no.	Change
Aug	1-0117053	Front axle – front and rear reinforced double-acting telescopic shock absorbers
Aug	1-0117700	Armrest on left-hand door discontinued
Aug		Tank filler cap – sealing strengthened, locking spring reinforced and stamped with VW emblem
Sep	1-0119588	0.05mm greater piston clearance on No. 3 cylinder
Sep	1-0120959	Radially ribbed clutch disc
Sep	1-0123476	Right track rod – left- and right-hand thread, standard
Oct	1-0127560	Reinforced clutch lever
Oct	1-0128058	Larger roller for accelerator mechanism
Oct	1-0128116	Driver's seat left runner raised by 15mm
Oct		Starting handle discontinued
Dec	1-0136729	Pushrod tubes – corrugations only at cylindrical ends

ID plate in spare wheel well – body number stamped into metal below. From 1950 'Made in Germany' plate added below body number.

1950

Export and Standard models with Golde cloth manually folding sunroof. Cloth had four square corners; Golde name appeared on handle (production started 28 April 1950; chassis number 1-0162580).

Date	Chassis no.	Change
Jan	1-0138765	Oil can be drained completely from crankcase. Oil level 2.51 – oil splashguard dropped. Main bearing No. 4 with groove
Jan	1-0138835	Torsion bars – upper and lower level – five-leaf
Jan	1-0140130	Larger knob fitted to boot-lock cable
Jan	1-0140243	Gasket between cylinder and cylinder head
Jan	1-0140537	Warning lights on dashboard – left, indicator and main beam – right, generator plus oil-warning light
Jan	1-0141601	Phosphated and blackened dipstick
Jan	1-0143276	Sealing ring between headlights and front wings
Feb		19mm hexagonal head on oil drain plug (some vehicles)
Feb	1-0146222	Accelerator cable – pin and clip at front
Mar		Revised solid VW insignia – letters 'V' and 'W', with space between
Mar	1-0155020	Headlights by Bosch – formerly VW
Mar	1-0156129	Tailpipe diameter 32mm – previously 31mm
Apr	1-0156991	Introduction of cut-outs in tops of door windows, allowing draught-free ventilation. Window raiser design amended
Apr	1-0158253	Export model and Cabriolet: hydraulic brakes standard; some cars fitted with hydraulic brakes in March, from chassis 1-0155322
Apr	1-0159782	Locking handle – right door
Apr	1-0161234	Hinged float fitted to Solex carburettor
Apr	1-0162444	T-shaped turn handle for heater control positioned behind handbrake lever (pull up, turn 90 degrees to lock)
May	1-0162580	Engine cooling manual control valve with swivel handle replaced by automatic bellows thermostat
May	1-0164402	Connecting pipe on exhaust box now standard
May	1-0164460	Brake fluid reservoir – with float rather than filter
May		Mahle Autothermic piston fitted on some cars

Rear Windows

ABOVE: Pre-October 1952 – Export or Standard (no bright trim inserts).

ABOVE RIGHT: October 1952–March 1953, Export model with bright trim insert.

RIGHT: March 1953–July 1957, Export model.

FAR LEFT: March 1953–July 1957, Standard model, no trim.

LEFT: August 1957–July 1964, Export model.

ABOVE LEFT: August 1957–July 1964, Standard model, no trim.

ABOVE: August 1964–July 1967 and beyond, Deluxe, 1300 and 1500.

LEFT: August 1964–July 1967 and beyond, 1200A – base model.

1950

Date	Chassis no.	Change
May	1-0167890	Hydraulic brake master cylinder reduced from 22.2mm to 19.5mm – rear wheel brake cylinders from 19.05mm to 15.9mm
May		Heating channels – noise suppressed
Jun	1-0169714	Ashtrays – dashboard and rear-right side-panel
Jun	1-0173719	Single-spring clutch now standard
Aug	1-0183539	Hardened exhaust valves – standard
Oct	1-0202071	Shorter handbrake lever

1951

The year of the infamous crotch-cooler ventilation system, the birth of the Wolfsburg Crest
bonnet badge and the first attempt at brightwork, which was set into the windscreen rubber.

Date	Chassis no.	Change
Jan	1-0221051	Modified generator pulley – to stop V-belt jumping off
Jan	1-0221638	Opening flaps for ventilation built into front quarter panels – invariably known now as 'crotch-coolers'
Jan	1-0224763	Sleeve for guiding return spring on accelerator cable
Jan	1-0225376	Crankcase made of Elektron (formerly a re-melt alloy)
Mar		Distributor marked with number and letter, indicating month and year respectively
Mar	1-0241734	Camshaft gear built from Resitax, a synthetic material – Export model only
Mar	1-0242600	Silencer – pipe modified
Apr	1-0243731	Badge fitted between polished aluminium boot handle and central boot trim; represents part of the coat of arms of Count von Schulenburg; reddish brown wolf standing between the turrets of white castle against a blue background; mounted on polished aluminium base; known for many years as the Wolfsburg Crest
Apr	1-0243731	Front heater flaps moved inside heat exchangers
Apr	1-0244003	Double-acting telescopic shock absorbers replaced rear single-acting lever type on Export and Cabriolet
Apr	1-0244668	Bright trim polished aluminium insert in rubber seal around windscreen – 8mm in diameter; held with thirty-six clips
Apr	1-0241638	Bonnet released by Bowden cable – previously handle
		Cabriolet only – lockable glove compartment, pocket on both door trim panels, additional door switch
Apr	1-0246090	Generator RED 130/6-2600 AL16 (previously AL15)
Jul	1-0272406	Rubber boot fitted to handbrake lever
Aug	1-0276126	Ventilation flaps – new mesh screen and operating lever
Sep	1-0287416	Wheel bolts no longer included in tool kit
Oct	1-0296592	Jacking points strengthened
Nov	1-0304210	Bolster cushions on rear seats discontinued
Dec	1-0308653	Dashboard indicator lamp 6V 0.6W; previously 1.2W

1952

October sees a revised Export model with additional brightwork, completely redesigned dashboard (also applicable to the Standard model),
plus synchromesh on all forward gears except first.

All cars run on smaller but fatter tyres – the new Beetles are sometimes referred at as 'oval dash splits' or Zwitters.

Date	Chassis no.	Change
Jan	1-0316900	Boot on chassis tunnel of handbrake lever (Export only)
Feb	1-0324758	Hydraulic brake reservoir without float
Mar	1-0338059	Connecting pipe between tailpipe and silencer discontinued
May	1-0357667	One spring replaced previous two valve ones
Jun	1-0365201	Diameter reduced on clutch-cable adjusting nut; operating lever with conical eye
Jun	1-0365716	'Door' in luggage compartment, only accessible with carpet and rails removed, giving access to clutch-cable adjuster and transmission fill plug – discontinued
Aug	1-0382029	Oil bath air filter fitted to some models
01/10/52	1-0397023	Total redesign of dashboard: starter button to left of steering wheel on face of dash – previously to right; speedometer directly above steering column; central location rectangular grille hiding optional speaker (chrome-plated on Export, painted on Standard); directly below grille blanking panel for optional radio; between grille and glovebox, small rectangular ashtray – initially no handle to ease opening; rectangular glovebox, with hinged door and push button to open

specification detail changes month by month

Date	Chassis no.	Change
01/10/52	1-0397023	Speedometer redesigned – rest or zero at bottom left, milometer below centre of needle (previously above); max speed shown at 120km/h (80mph) – no change; bottom centre – indicator 'arrows', red when in use; initially two separate 'arrows' changed in March 1953 to one combined; either side small warning lights for oil pressure (red) and generator (green); bright trim surrounding gauge on Export model
		Lights and wiper switch – left side of radio blanking panel – pull-out switch for each (previously rotary)
		Choke control (ivory-coloured knob on Export) to right of radio blanking panel (previously on tunnel by gearlever)
		Broader demister vents by windscreen
		Rectangular interior light above left door pillar (previously round and above split rear-window panes); switch to operate initially remote – positioned under dashboard near steering column
		Heating adjustable by rotary knob behind handbrake lever stamped with directional arrows; stamped H, plus A and Z (H = *Heizklappenzug* – heater control, A = *Auf* – open, Z = *Zu* – close); lettering dropped from USA cars within short period but remained on European Export models
		Rear ashtray now rectangular – bright, ribbed with small ivory pull handle (previously circular)
		Intake manifold fitted with pre-heating tube in aluminium casting
		Carburettor Solex 28 PCI (previously 26 VFIS)
		Torsion bars six-leaf (previously five-leaf); torsion bar diameter reduced from 25mm to 24mm
		Shock-absorber travel increased from 90mm to 130mm
		Synchromesh gearing on 2nd, 3rd, 4th (Export and Cabriolet)
		Rubber/steel gearbox mountings added front and rear
		Tyres – 5.60 × 15, wheel rims 4J × 15 (previously 5.00 × 16)
		Rear brake cylinders 17.5mm (previously 15.9mm)
		Quarter lights on doors. Vertical 'pillars' separated quarter light and main window – chromed on Export, bright aluminium on Cabriolet and painted on Standard
		Three and a quarter turns to raise or lower crank-operated window (previously ten and a half turns
		T-handle replaced vertical handle on engine lid (optional lockable)
		Noise reduction padding behind engine in engine bay
		Bumpers redesigned – heavier and wider; centre indentation deleted. Overriders curved and heftier (chromed on Export and Cabriolet model; painted on Standard)
		Standard model horn relocated behind wing (like Export). Cut-out in wing and grille, but no matching dummy grille in other front wing – painted
		Horn grille and mock grille changed to oval shape from round and made slightly larger. Dummy grille – black metal masking plate beneath, with cut-out in wing under it, thereby matching wing with horn behind
		8mm polished aluminium metal trim added to all remaining windows; seal modified – no clips required
		Bonnet-mounted insignia made from pressed rather than cast aluminium, plus hollow or cut-out. Four mounting tabs to hold it in place
		New smaller, shallower centre light casing at rear, creased in centre, bulb and plastic lens hidden underneath unlike previous 'Pope's nose'; function restricted to illumination of licence plate
		New oval-shaped rear lights with chrome-plated ring around rear-facing lens. In the top of the metal housing was an upside-down heart-shaped cut-out – hence popular nickname of heart-shaped tail light. 'Heart' lens – brake-light function; oval lens – night-light function
		Steering wheel colour changed from Ivory to Grey Beige. On Deluxe Beetles for Export centre horn button black with Wolfsburg Crest in gold; home market Deluxe model remained ivory but Crest in gold added
		Rectangular rear view mirror reshaped – more rounded at corners
		Fuse box for brake/tail light on reverse of dashboard
		Windscreen wiper – wider sweep, more power and self-parking (Export model only)
		Intermittent fitting of fuel tanks with 60mm filler neck and cap – but 100mm remained most common
		Battery 70Ah (previously 84Ah); strap longitudinal, previously at right angles to length of car
		Change to trim – boot, side and running boards (Export model); smooth appearance – rib deleted, non-corrosive alloy, polished and anodized. Base of Wolfsburg Crest modified – top wider, anodized finish
Nov		Flame trap on felt cone air filter

ABOVE: *Close-up of pre-April 1951 windscreen – note wiper arms, 2mm round steel (spec to 1954).*
LEFT: *Pre-April 1951 windscreen – no trim on Export or Standard.*

ABOVE: *Close-up of Export model windscreen April 1951–July 1957 – note flat wiper arms (spec 1954 onwards).*
LEFT: *April 1951–July 1957 windscreen – trim insert on Export model.*

August 1957–July 1964, windscreen Export model with trim insert.

August 1957–July 1964, windscreen Standard model – no trim.

ABOVE: *August 1964–July 1967 and beyond, windscreen Deluxe model, 1300 and 1500 with trim insert.*
RIGHT: *August 1964–July 1967 and beyond, windscreen 1200A base model.*

1953

Two significant changes occur during the year, the first taking place in March with the removal of the bar between the two rear pieces of glass and the creation of a new oval-shaped window.

The second change occurred in December, when the 25bhp engine was replaced by a more powerful 30bhp unit.

Date	Chassis no.	Change
Jan	1-0428221	Clamping strap on oil-bath air filter
Jan	1-0433397	Air correction jet on carburettor 200 (previously 190)
		Ball check-valves bronze (previously steel)
Jan	1-0435509	Valve clearance 10mm (previously 15mm)
Feb	1-0441708	Adjustable door striker plate (previously not so)
10/03/53	1-0454951	Slightly curved oval rear window replaced the two flat panes of the split-window Beetle – 23 per cent increase in size; safety glass replaced plate glass; trim anodized aluminium
		Ashtray now has handle
		Interior light fitted with off switch. 10W bulb – previously 5W
		Semaphore indicator arrows on speedometer now one – previously two
Jun	1-0495968	Hole for windscreen wiper shaft 8mm deeper
		Boot lid support shorter – altering and reducing angle of open lid
Jul	1-0503371	Door quarter lights with fasteners with push-in button lock – previously without button
Aug	1-0517304	Front torsion bars increased from six to eight leaves
Aug	1-0517880	Front wheel-bearing caps no longer filled with grease
Nov	1-0552991	Heater knob inscription deleted (Standard model)
21/12/53	1-0575415	New 30bhp engine
		Brake fluid reservoir behind spare wheel instead of on brake master cylinder
		Front heater vents enlarged – becoming oval with wire mesh – trim also oval; rear vents discontinued at same time
Dec	1-0575417	Dynamo uprated from 130W to 160W
		Instrument illumination automatic and can be regulated
		Interior light now worked with door contacts – three-way setting
		Windscreen wipers – flat section arms, herringbone section blades and arms, painted silver-grey (previously chromed)
		Fan belt narrower, with synthetic fibre insert instead of rubber cord
		Starter button discontinued, as starter function integrated into key switch (button smaller, dash-mounted in final period)
		Battery clamp strap – new type with over-centre catch (previously secured with springs)

Headlight glass

ABOVE: Headlight VW glass, Hella.
ABOVE RIGHT: Sealed beam headlight as per US spec cars from April 1955. Clear glass – parking light visible.
RIGHT: Headlight VW glass (asymmetrical beam type from August 1960).

Headlight VW glass, Hella with adjusting screws at 5 and 7 o'clock.

1954

The main changes for 1954 had in reality occurred at the end of 1953, although the USA would see the disappearance of the heart-shaped tail light in October, while semaphore casings were smooth, lacking rivets on the casings and ribs on the lenses. Cabriolets from this year onwards received a dash-mounted passenger grab handle (not fitted on the Export model until the 1961 model year).

Date	Chassis no.	Change
Jan	1-0591433	Integral loop handle and cap – dipstick
Feb	1-0518795	Oil cooler marked with month and year on the underside
Mar	1-0607509	Flywheel seal, aluminium foil (previously paper seal)
Mar	1-0611493	Petrol tank cap galvanized throughout with hydronalium
Mar	1-0623266	Diameter of front and rear brake hoses 12.2mm (previously 10mm)
Apr	1-0637872	Distributor VJU 4BR 3mk – improved springs for bobweights
May	1-0645501	Brake cylinders – four mounting bolts (previously two)
Jul	1-0678201	Filter mesh discontinued on oil filler cap
Aug	1-0696501	Spare fan belt no longer included in tool kit
Aug	1-0702742	Compression raised on 30bhp engine
		Rotor arm with groove for dust protection
		Distributor VJU 4 BR 8 and VJ BR 8
Oct	1-0722916	Heart-shaped tail light discontinued in USA and Canada – now a double-filament bulb; lens dark-red plastic and curved outwards; previously rear lens made of violet-red glass and flat
Oct	1-0730023	Windscreen shatterproof – clear-view area in front of the driver
Oct	1-0734000	Water-drainage hole at base of tail light housing
Dec	1-0770501	Oil slot for door-hinge pin lubrication (previously oil hole)

1955

1955 saw Volkswagen change its model year policy. Having more or less clung to calendar years previously, VW adopted the US style of model year, offering the 1956 Beetle from August 1955, after the annual factory holidays.

The changes itemized below relate to cars produced between January and the end of July 1955. For the first time, there was a significant parting of the way between European market and USA/Canadian Beetles.

Date	Chassis no.	Change
Apr		USA and Canadian models fitted with sealed beam headlamps – clear outer lens making parking/side light bulb visible
Apr	1-0847967	Flashing wing-mounted indicators optional extra for USA and Canadian markets replacing semaphores (Standard not affected as not exported to USA or Canada)
Apr	1-0860576	Number plate light casing amended – small crease deleted – housing both rounded and smooth
Apr		USA and Canada only – slim cylindrical bar added to front and rear bumpers; front continuous with outward curve to allow easy opening of boot; rear – two separate rails with gap in centre to allow opening of engine lid; rails passed through enlarged overriders
		Support braces either side of front valance – front, through each wing – rear; purpose – to line up with average USA-manufactured car bumper; became very popular accessory on European-market Beetles, which continued with original style of bumper until the end of the 1967 model year in the case of the Cabriolet and Deluxe; commonly known as 'towel-rail bumpers' by enthusiasts
May	1-0871207	All USA and Canadian Beetles equipped with flashing indicators; mounted by headlamps outside; cone-shaped with flat front to clear lens; base painted in body colour of car; unit made by Hella; often referred to as 'bullet-shape' indicators today
May		Tail light increased in both size and appearance for USA and Canadian market cars. Lens taller, creating more of an oval shape; lens bevelled at edge – flat – made out of glass; bulbs signalled stop, turn and tail light functions
May		USA and Canada – rear valance amended to accommodate twin tailpipes by inserting two indentations at the base
		New exhaust sat 18mm higher than previously, while tailpipes were 38mm higher than previous single pipe; also chromed
May	1-0881293	Gear lever assembly on synchromesh and non-synchromesh models now identical
Jun	1-0904566	Ignition/starter switch – lock number on fixing lug
Jul	1-0927373	Number plate light now K6V/10W (previously L6V/5W)

1956 – Beetles built between 1 August 1955–31 July 1956

While not as extensive as the changes made to the Beetle in October 1952, the introduction of a new model year policy also heralded a reasonable number of design changes.

Date	Chassis no.	Change
4/8/55	1-0929746	Twin tailpipes adopted on all Beetles (see May 1955); standard model pipes not chromed, but painted black; exhaust box – single chamber
		Spark plugs now 225T1s – previously 175T1
		Fuel tap without mesh filter and switch position altered
		New shape of steering wheel; the two spokes were placed off-centre to improve driver visibility of gauge; colour now grey-beige (Ivory 1955 and 1954 – grey-beige Oct 1952 to end 1953); new smaller centre horn, with black button and Wolfsburg Crest of simpler design than previously – not interchangeable with earlier model
		Torsion bars setting 12 degrees + 30 (previously 13 degrees + 30)
		Handbrake cable bolted to handbrake lever, previously on the actuating arm (Export and Cabriolet only)
		Heater knob relocated further forwards – to the right of and slightly forwards behind the gear lever (now in front of the handbrake); gear-lever design altered to accommodate this change

Indicators

ABOVE: Semaphore with ribbed surface and visible rivets – in action; pre-1954.
RIGHT: Pre-1954 semaphore with visible rivets.

1954 and onwards semaphore with plain surface – in action.

1954 and onwards semaphore.

May 1955–July 1957 – US-spec bullet-style indicator.

US indicator introduced in August 1957.

From August 1960 all cars had wing-mounted indicators.

Some markets demanded clear lenses.

From 31 October 1963, the indicator became bigger – less like a teardrop in shape.

Date	Chassis no.	Change
4/8/55	1-0929746 (cont.)	Gear lever cranked (previously straight – *see* above)

Front seats 30mm wider; backrest now adjustable to three positions; seat rails – number of adjustments available increased from two to seven; runners no longer ran parallel to the floor, but were higher at the front and sloped downwards at the rear; seat front legs shorter

Fuel tank modified – flatter at top and deeper at the bottom (*see* point below); filler cap reduced in size to 80mm

Boot increased in size to 85ltr (previously 70ltr)

Luggage compartment behind rear seat decreased in size from 130ltr down to 120ltr, primarily due to redesign of rear seat (metal luggage rails in the boot had been discontinued in August 1954)

Centre tunnel carpeting discontinued in favour of rubber matting (Export and Deluxe only – Standard always had rubber)

Boot lid handle and lock improved but no visible change; release knob for bonnet inside car moved further to the left

Trim inlay in window rubbers reduced from 8mm to 7mm in diameter

Plastic grab handles replaced cloth. Cloth trimmed door panels now with leatherette strip and bright trim

European model rear lights now like USA in style and design – all models, tail lights moved up wings by 60mm, mainly to increase visibility on US cars with larger overriders and so on

Tail lights

Early 1949 tail light with lens mounted on a metal base.

Late 1949 tail light with aluminium trim ring – trim deleted 1950–October 1952.

Tail light October 1952 until July 1955 most markets, but only until October 1954 US market.

Nicknamed the heart-shaped tail light for an obvious reason.

Tail light, all markets, August 1955–May 1961 (from August 1960 – three-purpose unit).

ABOVE: From August 1955, the all-market tail light was positioned 2cm higher on the wing.
FAR LEFT: May 1961–July 1967 – three-section rear light.
LEFT: Three-section light, US spec – all red lenses.

specification detail changes month by month

Date	Chassis no.	Change
4/8/55	1-0929746 (cont.)	Battery 66Ah (previously 70Ah)
		Spark plugs 225T1 (previously 175T1)
		Dynamo pulley nut reduced in size from 36mm to 21mm
		36mm ring spanner discontinued in tool kit; 21mm spanner for spark plugs could now be used for dynamo pulley nut
		Cabriolet rear window – new larger shape and encased in bright metal trim
Feb 56	1 113 449	Centrifugal and vacuum curve in distributor set 3 to 5 degrees lower in upper speed range
Mar		Ground clearance less – 155mm (previously172mm) (Export model)
Apr	1 149 147	Padding for front seats – horsehair and rubber – made 15mm thicker
Apr	1 165 108	Distance from centre of petrol tank to centre of filler neck reduced – now 215mm (previously 245mm)
Jun	1 210 230	Vacuum pipe relocated underneath accelerator cable (previously above choke cable)
Jul	1 248 030	Tubeless tyres now fitted to all Beetles (Cabriolet two days earlier)

Central rear light

Unique KdF-Wagen central light housing.

LEFT: Pre-October 1952 central rear light housing – known as a 'Pope's nose'.
ABOVE: The 'Pope's nose' combined the function of brake light and licence plate illumination.

Post-October 1952 number plate light housing.

From March 1955 the housing became more rounded, losing its top central crease.

From August 1957 a flat bulb cover was replaced by the style of housing depicted.

ABOVE: From August 1966 the shape of the engine lid was amended to make the licence plate sit closer to vertical. The number plate housing was adapted accordingly.
LEFT: From August 1963 the shape of the engine lid and the number plate cover was amended, the latter becoming much larger.

1957 – Beetles built between 1 August 1956–31 July 1957

Changes were restricted to minor improvements.

Date	Chassis no.	Change
Aug 56	1 257 230	New lock plate with adjustable wedge on certain cars. Previously non-adjustable (not universal)
Aug	1 266 678	Light alloy camshaft timing gear (previously Resitex)
Sep		VW emblem on hubcaps now only painted in black
Sep	1 283 328	Brass pins and studs for hood (previously steel) (Cabriolet)
Oct	1 320 179	Steering column splined shaft – changed from twenty-four to forty-eight teeth – Export/Cabriolet only (Standard from June 1957 – chassis number 1 568 040)
Oct	1 329 017	Home market – all cars fitted with external mirror
Oct	1 326 040	Lubrication nipple on door discontinued on Cabriolet
Jan 57	1 394 163	Heater vent in front footwells moved back by around 10cm
Feb	1 423 927	Windscreen wiper motor with permanent magnetic brake
		Number plate light fixed higher, with diffusing lens, to improve illumination
Feb	1 444 260	Golde sunroof became longer – 1,380mm (previously 1,350mm)

Trim and horn

ABOVE: From June 1949 and launch of Export Beetle – circular grille on both front wings; one was decorative, the other was to cover the hole created to allow the horn to sound clearly.
ABOVE RIGHT: Standard model horn retained in front of wing – no decorative or functional grilles.
LEFT: Horn on Standard stayed on view until October 1952.

ABOVE: October 1952–July 1967; Export/Deluxe, 1300 and 1500 all featured two oval grilles – one on each front wing.

RIGHT: Standard model – one grille only post October 1952. Decorative grille omitted, leaving unadorned wing.

Bumpers and overriders

Some pre-1949 cars had plain bumpers and banana-style overriders.

Home market Standard model – October 1952 onwards, silvery painted bumper.

June 1949–October 1952, Export model – grooved bumper and small overrider.

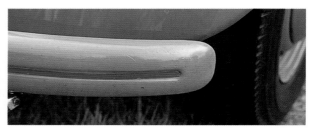

ABOVE: June 1949–October 1952, Standard model – painted grooved bumper
RIGHT: October 1952–July 1967 – Export/Deluxe, 1300 and 1500 bumper and overrider.
BELOW LEFT: Export market Standard model, October 1952 onwards, chromed bumper.

ABOVE RIGHT: From late April 1955 onwards, all US bumpers had an additional bar above the main bumper, supported by extended overriders. This feature quickly became a popular accessory for other markets.
LEFT: Rear US market bumper – note 'buttress' support and extended overrider.

Early cars featured a starting-handle bracket – discontinued October 1949.

1958 – Beetles built between 1 August 1957–31 July 1958

Oval window production finished on 31 July 1957 – chassis number 1 600 439.

For the new model year the Beetle was launched with more modifications than had been the case since October 1952. Most striking was the much larger rear window and a dashboard that in its basic appearance would remain in production until worldwide Beetle production ceased in July 2003.

Date	Chassis no.	Change
1/8/57	1 600 440	Rear window curved and rectangular in shape; 95 per cent larger than the oval window it replaced
		Windscreen – increased at both the top and sides (window pillars made narrower); 17 per cent larger
		Rear-view mirror became larger and oval in shape; held with new style of bracket and offset
		Cabriolet rear window increased in size by 45 per cent; windscreen increased by 8 per cent (narrower pillars)
		New windscreen wiper arms with longer blades – wipers closer together, faster wiper action
		Air-intake slots below rear screen reduced in number due to increase in size of glass; fifty small slots replaced the previous two sets of twenty-one large slots; also improved water drainage, two new drainage holes
		Engine compartment lid redesigned – flatter, losing 'W' look
		Cabriolet lid – horizontal air vents (two banks of five) replaced vertical slots; new lid also had rain trap and drain under the vents
		Brightwork trim revamped with dimples at either side and rounded at centre
		Completely new and symmetrical dashboard layout. LHD cars – L to R: recessed speaker grille; speedometer gauge and steering column; small recessed grille to balance first-mentioned grille – both trimmed from rear with painted fibre screen; radio blanking panel positioned dead centre. Above left headlamp switch – pull out for on and turn to right for brighter illumination of dash gauge. Above right wiper switch – below central pull-out ashtray with ivory-coloured knob. Plus choke pull and ignition switch (closest to driver); glovebox – shape imitated that of speaker grille and dummy grille

Hubcaps

Cogwheel-style hubcap on a KdF-Wagen.

Cogwheel-style hubcap on a Kübelwagen.

More usual painted nipple hubcap – pre-June 1949.

ABOVE: Usual post-June 1949 hubcap, until July 1965; note size reduced October 1952 when wheel changed from 16in to 15in. Wheel colour-ways amended over years and colour-co-ordinated painted VW symbol – then black and finally no paint.
LEFT: Domed hubcap with black painted logo – 1957 models to July 1963.
RIGHT: From August 1965 the flat hubcap and perforated steel wheel fitted to the VW 1500 (Type 3) replaces the Beetle's 'solid' wheel and domed hubcap.

Nipple-style hubcap as fitted to a 1948 Beetle (chrome unusual).

specification detail changes month by month

Date	Chassis no.	Change
		Bright cast-metal trim with lugs at rear ran centrally across the dashboard of the Export model in four sections; nuts screwed onto lugs to hold in place; glovebox – inside or reverse three ivory-coloured plastic plugs, which when removed give access to screws holding trim in place
		Speedometer trim ring modified – not interchangeable with earlier models
		Accelerator pedal, now traditional oblong rubber-covered treadle (previously roller)
		Rear torsion bars – internal splines shortened
		USA and Canadian Beetles only – new style of flashing front indicator positioned centrally on top of wings – unit rounded at the front, tapered at rear; chrome-plated housing – clear lens
Nov	1 709 421	Acid level 5mm over top of plates, previously 10–15mm
Jan 58	1 789 907	Magnetic drain plugs on engine and gearbox (previously without)
Jan	1 802 775	28PCI carburettor; spring for idling screw now 12mm (previously 13.5mm)
Feb	1 832 100	Rubber seal ring replaces wax-dipped felt gasket at top of steering
Mar		Sparkplug spanner with rubber sleeve (previously with retaining spring)
Apr		Wing/bodywork, wing/running board, horn fixing bolts – 13mm hexagonal (previously 14mm)
Apr	1 925 488	Steering wheel pin bush bronze – rolled and slit sideways
May	1 938 979	Kingpin thrust washer now white plastic (previously fibre)
Jun	1 975 105	Plastic – nylon – Venturi tube on 28PCI carburettor (previously light alloy)
Jun	1 994 320	Distributor rotor and sparkplug caps remotely suppressed

1959 – Beetles built between 1 August 1958–31 July 1959

Few changes making the introduction of a padded sun visor, replacing the previous transparent plastic affair, on the Export model a highlight.

Date	Chassis no.	Change
Sep 58	2 071 106	Cable pull handle moved closer to steering column
Dec	2 217 270	Brake master cylinder secured with hexagonal bolts and spring washer, previously studs with nuts
Jan 59	2 245 160	Hub cap removing hook in tool kit
Jan	2 252 455	New padded vinyl sun visor, previously transparent green plastic. Passenger sun visor part of standard equipment on Export (neither change applicable to the Standard model)
Jan	2 256 907	Steering tie rods on RHD cars modified – left tie rod 807mm (previously 814mm); right tie rod 325mm (previously 318mm)
Jan	2 269 017	Filler cap changed to vent fumes through a diaphragm (previously a labyrinth system)
Mar	2 317 671	Cabriolet rear seat modified – more padding and softer
Apr	2 368 910	Sparkplugs now 175 (previously 225)
May	2 409 056	Modified heater junction box
May	2 425 182	Silencer/heat exchanger and silencer/tailpipe conical asbestos rings and clamps
May	2 428 094	Stub pipes on silencer shortened by 10mm
Jul	2 503 092	Heat resistant fan belt as standard; five to eight belt pulley spacers (previously eight to eleven)

1960 – Beetles built between 1 August 1959–31 July 1960

A new steering wheel, redesigned Wolfsburg Crest bonnet badge and revised
door handles head the list of changes to identify a 1960 model year Beetle.

Date	Chassis no.	Change
6/8/59	2 528 668	Distance from tip of dipstick to upper oil level reduced by 4mm to 40mm
		Dished steering wheel with chrome-plated semi-circular horn ring; Wolfsburg Crest remained at the centre; colour – Stone Beige (Standard model retained black three-spoke affair dating back to 1949); Cabriolet from 2 533 099
		Steering column with ball bearing mounted in outer tube
		More rigid chromed external door handles with push button, previously pull handle; key slot vertical for one year only, then horizontal (see 1/8/60); door lock and striker plate modified, requiring less pressure to close
		Arm rest modified – hollowed out, as it was before August 1955 – purpose to act as door pull
		Indicator arm switch – now self-cancelling
		Rubber stops to make action quieter on semaphores
		Fuse for dipped beam lights in front fuse box
		Front seat passenger footrest –sheet metal painted black and covered in rubber as part of the general floor covering
		Plastic-covered inserts – heel boards – under the rear seat
		Front seat backrests more steeply angled, with deeper curve

VW insignia and Wolfsburg Crest badge

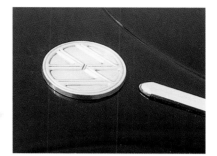

FAR LEFT: Wolfsburg Crest badge as fitted to Export model April 1951–July 1959 (base modified in October 1952).
LEFT: Simplified Wolfsburg Crest badge as fitted to Export model – August 1959 until discontinued in October 1962.
RIGHT: Solid aluminium VW bonnet insignia Export model – version 2 (March 1950–October 1952); earlier version June 1949 onwards also solid, but 'V' and 'W' touched at centre.

Hollow VW bonnet insignia Export model, October 1952– September 1962.

VW bonnet insignia Export model October 1962 onwards.

Early ventilation

LEFT: Ventilation flap added to front quarter panels in January 1951 – revised to include mesh (as illustrated) August 1951 and discontinued in October 1952. Known as 'crotch-coolers'.
BELOW: The quarter light introduced in October 1952 remained a feature on all Beetles to the end of the period covered by this book and beyond (car shown 1967 1200).

ABOVE LEFT: Curved cut-out added in April 1950 to improve ventilation (until October 1952).
LEFT: Quarter-light catches changed over the years – the Standard model had painted catches, while they were chromed on the Export models.

Date	Chassis no.	Change
		Anti-roll bar at front – pivot point of swing axles lowered by around 15 per cent by tilting both the engine and the gearbox forwards by 2 degrees
		Redesigned Wolfsburg Crest bonnet badge – simplified design, consisting of red Wolf, bright castle, blue waves on black background
Aug	2 528 890	Generator 180W, previously 160W
Aug	2 539 142	Trim mouldings sealed with rubber caps from outside (previously caps fixed on inside of body panels)
Aug	2 575 176	Quarter-light frame reinforced
Sep	2 577 839	Cabriolet – door buffer fitted under door catch
Sep	2 616 071	Cabriolet – felt matting fitted on bottom of luggage space behind rear seat to deaden sound
Oct	2 668 581	8mm hexangular socket for adjusting link pins (previously flush at both ends)
Nov	2 708 099	Cork seal on fuel tap (previously Thiokol)
Jan 60		Valve clearance adjusting nut 13mm (previously 14mm)
Mar	2 921 552	Hardened face on trailing arm outer needle bearing
		Steering damper located between long tie rod and axle tube
May	3 060 711	Plastic warm air ducts incorporate silencer between bodywork and engine (previously metal)

specification detail changes month by month

Engine lid handles

FAR LEFT: *Export handle – chromed; lock optional, 1949–October 1952.*

ABOVE LEFT: *Standard handle – painted, no lock, closed position, 1949–October 1952.*

ABOVE: *Export chromed T-shaped handle, October 1952–July 1964.*

FAR LEFT: *Standard home-market painted T-shaped handle – more often painted silver, October 1952–July 1964.*

LEFT: *Push-button handle, August 1964–July 1967 and beyond.*

Boot lid handles

FAR LEFT: *Polished aluminium handle, May 1949–October 1952.*
LEFT: *Detail of the base of the handle, May 1949–October 1952.*
RIGHT: *Post-October 1952 handle – Export model and so on; slight changes made in 1956 (this example dates from 1957).*
MIDDLE LEFT: *Home-market Standard handle, dating from 1955 – painted; more often in silvery colour.*

BOTTOM LEFT: *From May 1949 onwards the boot lid was released via a pull handle under the dash; Export model pictured; Standard models were black.*

Door handles

RIGHT: *Standard model painted handle – smooth, pre-August 1955.*
MIDDLE RIGHT: *Export model chromed handle – smooth, pre-August 1955.*
FAR RIGHT: *Standard model – silvery painted handle, ridged, August 1955–July 1959.*
RIGHT: *Export model chromed handle – ridged, August 1955–July 1959.*
MIDDLE RIGHT: *Push-button stationary handle, August 1959–July 1966.*
FAR RIGHT: *August 1966–July 1967, only door handle.*

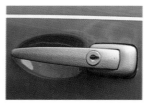

Engine lids

RIGHT: Pre-July 1949, W-shaped engine lid – this car dates from 1946.
FAR RIGHT: Close-up of a pre-July 1949 lid, with pressing for the licence plate.

FAR LEFT: Post-July 1949 W-shaped lid – used until August 1957 (as pre-July 1949 but without the pressing).
LEFT: Slightly modified W-shaped lid – post-October 1952 due to the smaller number plate light housing.

August 1957–July 1963, flatter appearance of lid, squared-off below the number plate – usually referred to as semi-W lid.

ABOVE: August 1966, redesigned lid without any sort of W look. Slightly humped to make the number plate sit almost vertically (US requirement).
LEFT: August 1963–July 66, lid further amended to accommodate larger-size number plate light housing.

Sunroof

Made by Golde, the rubberized canvas sunroof introduced in April 1950 was available until July 1967 on Standard models and until August 1963 for Export cars. Its shape changed slightly over the years – this example can be dated to after May 1956 thanks to its rounded rear corners. PVC or vinyl material replaced the rubberized canvas on Export models in November 1955.

ABOVE: Sunroof open (from the front).
RIGHT: A chrome-plated lever opened the sunroof – the inside of the sunroof was trimmed in the same material as the rest of the headliner.

specification detail changes month by month

Although visibly the changes between the 1960 and 1961 model year Beetles were few, in reality the newer car exhibited a considerable number of advances to anyone caring to scour the vehicle's specification.

Date	Chassis no.	Change
1/8/60	3 192 507	New 34bhp engine for Export and Cabriolet Beetles (not Standard model) – air cleaner with intake air pre-heating to improve both idling and engine running at low speed
		New gearbox with redesigned one-piece casing; revised ratios on third and top gears (first – 3.80:1, second – 2.06:1, third – 1.32:1, fourth – 0.89:1, reverse – 3.88:1); synchromesh on all forward gears (not Standard model)
		Automatic choke – choke knob discontinued on dashboard (Export model)
		New design of exhaust – not interchangeable with earlier ones; only tailpipes carried over
		Rear suspension, rubber buffer lengthened by 10mm
		Captive threaded bush on front axle mounting extended by 7mm and mounting bolts moved backwards
		Door handle and lock barrel amended – slot horizontal, recessed and dust cover fitted
		Engine cover amended to accommodate new, longer, engine
		Standard model updated to plastic padded sun visor – remains single, plus driver's seat with adjustable backrest
		Oil pressure switch no longer adjustable
		Push on terminal for brake light switch, previously screw type
		Dip switch moved 10mm to the left
		Eight-circuit fuse box next to steering column, with transparent cover (previously located behind the dashboard cover in the boot)
		Speedometer reading now up to 140km/h (previously 120); intermediate markings discontinued
		Protective tube on steering cable discontinued
		Screen washer fitted with 1ltr-capacity screen-washer bottle located behind the spare wheel well; pressurized pump system operated by hand pump button at centre of wiper switch
		Small metal fitting – teardrop shaped behind VW insignia on cowl; through this windscreen-washer nozzle jets of water are directed to the screen
		Plastic brake fluid reservoir replaces metal canister
		Redesigned fuel tank – much flatter than previously, with filler on LH side (previously right); diameter of filler neck 60mm
		Redesigned fuel tank creates increased luggage space – 140ltr (previously 85ltr)
		Dash-mounted passenger grab handle now standard on Export model (previously only standard on Cabriolet)
		New rear ashtray, without handle
		Ignition starter switch – now non-repeat, requiring return to home position before starter can be operated once more
		Headlamps – asymmetrical dip beam, previously symmetrical – ensuring good light coverage even when on dipped headlights
		European models finally receive flashing wing-mounted front indicators (semaphores discontinued); narrow chrome-plated housings with amber/orange lenses; shape different to first USA-only wing-mounted front indicator; known today to some enthusiasts as the 'teardrop' indicator; Standard model received teardrop indicator housings but not chromed – instead painted (L266 Silver Grey)
Aug	3 223 145	New gasket for pre-heater tube left-hand connector flange, hole diameter 6mm (previously 16mm)
Aug	3 248 025	Ignition timing amended – 10 degrees before top dead centre (previously 7.5 degrees before top dead centre)
Oct	3 335 848	Boge shock absorbers at rear – 35 per cent softer
Oct	3 341 077	Boge shock absorbers at front – 26 per cent softer
Oct	3 405 001	Accelerator pedal – mounted higher and rubber extended at base
Jan 61	3 616 527	Thrust surface for distributor drive shaft 5mm deeper in left-hand half of crankcase
Jan	3 627 442	Fan pulley ratio 1.75:1 (previously 1.8:1)
Feb	3 672 005	Protective rubber cap for ignition lead discontinued
Mar	3 711 714	Door lock wedge made from plastic
Mar	3 712 664	Cabriolet – 4mm wider door-seal lip in latch area
Mar	3 771 255	Backrests of front seats fastened by crankpin with cap nut
May	3 856 472	Larger tail lights with amber section for indicator (home market); USA bound cars fitted with larger unit for start of '62 model year (chassis 4 010 995) – but lens all red (would remain so until end of '67 model year)
May	3 862 145	Red mark on speedometer dial marking 50 km/h point – no equivalent mph indication
May	3 924 800	Operating pressure for oil pressure switch 0.15-0.45 bar, previously 0.3-0.6 bar

1962 – Beetles built between 1 August 1961–31 July 1962

Although in reality the adoption across Europe of double-section tail lights – ensuring that the indicator function could be clearly spotted – was probably the most important improvement, the long overdue addition of a fuel gauge – at least on Export models – made the headlines amongst potential owners.

Date	Chassis no.	Change
31/7/61	4 010 995	Fuel gauge fitted to Export and Cabriolet models, dispensing with the need for a reserve fuel tap; located to the right of the speedometer on LHD cars and to the left with RHD models; square instrument trimmed with polished aluminium – in style of central dashboard trim; gauge indicates fuel level with or without ignition being turned on
		Steering – worm and roller, replacing worm and peg and making for better directional control and easier operation; tie rods adjustable both left and right (Home market – rest 30/8/61; not Standard)
		Heating outlets in driver's and front passenger's footwell now fitted with sliding shutters to aid demisting of windscreen (not Standard)
		Boards below rear seat fitted with circular warm air outlets (not Standard)
		Seat-belt mountings provided for driver and front seat passenger
		Seat rails lengthened to give 120mm adjustment range (previously 100mm; not Standard)
		New style of door retainer
		Spring-loaded strut on either side of the boot (previously single bonnet stay; not Standard model)
		Redesigned washer bottle – and change in operation from hand pump to pneumatic; dashboard button also redesigned – press centre rather than pull whole button in and out
Aug	4 036 536	Maintenance-free protection sleeves on handbrake cables (previously lubrication nipple)
Aug	4 057 923	Front seat backrest design amended to allow greater range of adjustment with cranked knob at base of seat frame
Aug	4 060 506	Grooved pin on new holding strap – door retainer
Oct	4 166 056	Operating temperature of thermostat reduced to 65–70° (previously 75–80°); automatic cooling air regulation
Nov	4 289 952	Knob on gear stick conical and smaller
Dec	4 357 893	Door-hinge pins treated with molybdenum and phosphated (previously oil-lubricated)
Jan 62	4 388 450	Rear wheel bearings – inner spacer ring thickness 5.9–6.1mm altered to 6.45–6.65mm
Jan	4 432 260	Fuel-pump operating lever as pressed part (previously two-part casing); pressure spring lengthened
Jan	4 420 885	Oil or wax paper stuck to inside of door panels; rubber seal on both window glass and lifter rail increased in length, improving water drainage.
Feb	4 519 277	Connecting pipe on the underside of the oil-bath air filter (previously on air intake – crankcase vent)
Apr	4 636 869	Fuel line between pump and carburettor – rubber tubing with braid covering, upgraded to pipe with flexible ends
Apr	4 630 938	Standard model – brake system upgraded from cable to hydraulic
Apr	4 671 926	Door hinges – number of bolts reduced from four to three and window regulator spring loaded in guide rail, 4 672 922
May	4 683 160	All clutch-pressure springs coloured brown (previously three yellow and three grey-blue)

ABOVE: *Pre-August 1955 cars featured a smooth rear valance and a single plain metal exhaust pipe.*
RIGHT: *Post-August 1955 cars featured twin tailpipes fitted around a revised valance with two 'cut-outs' – Export model had chrome pipes, Standard model painted black.*

specification detail changes month by month

1963 – Beetles built between 1 August 1962–31 July 1963

Although improvements to the Beetle were somewhat limited, the model year 1963 is notorious for the retrograde step of removing the simplified version of the Wolfsburg Crest bonnet badge from the car's list of fittings.

Date	Chassis no.	Change
30/7/62	4 846 836	Air filter on oil cooler, diameter of pre-heating pipe (induction manifold) at connecting flange was 25mm – now 27mm, shape of fan housing amended for greater efficiency; induction port on cylinder head now 27mm (previously 25mm)
		Handle for sliding roof now hinged and flatter
		Plastic window guides (previously fabric)
		White plastic headlining with polka-dot perforations replaces woollen material; easier to keep clean and makes car appear more spacious (initially made in pieces with separate centre section, but one-piece from 5 580 432)
		Insulation on floor plates – bitumen sheets now thicker
		Intermittent installation at first of new plastic oval-shaped windscreen washer nozzle
Aug	4 874 267	Oil fumes directed into oil bath air cleaner (previously released into open air)
Sep	4 978 442	Screw top replaces stopper on brake fluid reservoir
Sep	4 981 020	Vacuum pipe 375mm (previously 310mm)
Sep	4 988 623	New piston rings chamfered on the inner ring; grooves on two upper piston ring grooves reduced by 0.6mm
Oct	5 010 448	Wolfsburg Crest badge dropped from specification, with alloy trim extended accordingly, finishing closer to the boot handle; VW bonnet badge redesigned, now with three locating lugs – embossed circle on boot lid intended for mounting of VW badge
Dec	5 188 470	Rear passenger footwell heater vents – outlets fitted with regulating stick and knob
Dec	5 199 980	Heat exchangers fitted – sheet steel chambers with exhaust pipe from front cylinders through middle, air blown by the fan from a hose, air surrounding heat exchangers ducted through pipes to interior of car; exchangers reduce risk of fumes entering car; cars with heat exchangers can be identified through the two thick pipes leading off to the left and right of the fan housing; new design of exhaust to coincide with move to heat exchangers
		Plastic safety caps on spark-plug terminals
Jan 63	5 239 191	Inner sealing lip with spiral ring added to Hemscheidt steering damper
Jan	5 261 830	Clutch cable now 10mm shorter
Apr	5 419 871	Plastic seal around bumper bracket (previously rubber)
Apr	5 440 221	Contact surface of front seat back adjustment enlarged
Jun	5 578 122	Petrol injected into cylinders by 28 PICT carburettor increased to 1.4cc per accelerator pump stroke

1964 – Beetles built between 1 August 1963–31 July 1964

The easiest way to identify a 1964 model year Beetle is by its revised number plate light housing and by its chunkier, though less elegant, front indicator light housings – although this latter modification only came into place in October 1963.

Date	Chassis no.	Change
5/8/63	5 677 119	Steering wheel loses its semi-circular horn ring in favour of twin chromed thumb buttons standing proud of the two spokes of the wheel
		Hub caps – VW symbol at centre no longer picked out in black paint
		Rear tyre pressure – 1.7bar now recommended (previously 1.6)
		Standard model – steering wheel and control knobs now silver-beige, always black previously
		Standard model – roof material now plastic (previously woollen)
		Door seals now foam material
		Sunroof Export model (not Standard) crank-operated steel sunroof (previously folding fabric); much smaller opening with metal roof
		Engine lid curve slightly modified to accept much enlarged (wider) number plate light housing; bulb, socket and lens are identical to those of the VW 1500 – introduced in late 1961 (Standard not updated at this point)
		Amended internal operating mechanism for door locks
Sep	5 765 471	Single-tube shock absorbers with PVC synthetic protective sleeves; piston rods pull downwards
Oct	5 815 778	New sludge drainpipe with rubber vent on crankcase
Oct	5 875 847	Rear cut-out section for gear-change shaft coupling enlarged on upper part of chassis
Oct	5 888 185	Indicator housings widened, losing teardrop appearance in process
		Front wings and side panels – drillings amended due to repositioned indicator lights
Nov	5 909 656	Oil-bath air cleaner now has depression on lower part of filter due to enlarged automatic choke mechanism

Date	Chassis no.	Change
Dec	6 009513	Valve angle increased on rocker mechanism. Cylinder head pushrods and rockers modified; rocker shaft repositioned
Feb 64	6 130 478	Cabriolet – chromed steel trim for running board (previously aluminium)
Mar	6 223 768	Cover plate on oil filter fixed with cap nuts and copper washers (previously hexagon nuts and spring washers)
Apr	6 317 836	Two-piece battery hold-down strap – top release clip (previously, from 1956, clip at front near floor)
Jul	6 483 093	Cars now fully coated with wax preservative (previously part-treated)

RIGHT: Coloured rather than black running boards were often part of the specification in the 1960s.
FAR RIGHT: The jack was located in the boot throughout. Originally with a screw mechanism at the top, from March 1952 it was a pole with shimmy type mechanism. From August 1955, the jack was restrained by a metal 'strap'. Image shows post-August 1955 arrangement.

Petrol tanks and filler caps

RIGHT: From August 1949 the wire screen illustrated was an option.
FAR RIGHT: From October 1952 some cars were fitted with 60mm filler necks and caps (tank colour not original).

RIGHT: Most cars produced between October 1952–July 1955 had 100mm filler necks and caps.
FAR RIGHT: The style and shape of tank that was produced between August 1955–July 1960.

RIGHT: Fuel cap post August 1955 – 80mm diameter.
FAR RIGHT: From August 1960 the tank was much flatter and was carefully concealed under the boot card, with the filler protruding.

Dashboards

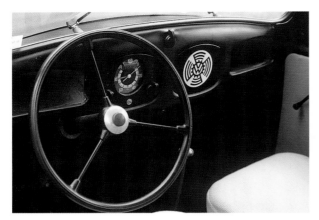

KdF-Wagen

1949–October 1952, Export model.

1949–October 1952, Standard model.

1949–October 1952, Karmann Cabriolet.

1949, Hebmüller.

October 1952–July 1957, Export (early example).

October 1952–July 1957, Export (later example).

August 1957, Export (early example – accessory rather than standard fuel gauge).

Dashboards

August 1957, Standard.

1957, Export (post-August 1961 – with fuel gauge).

August 1961 – for the '62 model year – a fuel gauge was added to the specification.

Until the end of July 1967, the fuel gauge remained separate from the other instrument functions on all Beetles.

1965 – Beetles built between 1 August 1964–31 July 1965

1965 Beetles are distinguishable by their larger windows all round, the appearance of a modern push-button catch on the engine lid and levers rather than a rotary knob to control the heater.

The Standard model made way for a new base model – the 1200A.

Date	Chassis no.	Change
3/8/64	115 000 001	Windscreen extended 28mm into roof panel (11 per cent bigger overall), rear window extended 20mm top to bottom and 10mm left to right (nearly 20 per cent larger); side windows, including quarter lights, larger due to slimmed-down pillars (rear side windows 18 per cent larger, front 6 per cent); windscreen slightly curved – sufficient to reduce glare; chromed metal between quarter light and front side window slanted rather than straight (painted on Standard model); window raiser now cable-operated (previously single arm); catch on quarter light minus push-button release
		Heater operated by lever positioned to the right of the rear section of the handbrake (previously rotary knob); rear vents operated by lever to the left of the rear section of the handbrake (previously controlled by individual sticks and knobs); main heater – red knob, rear vents – white knob (both flat when not in use and pulled upwards to use)
		Front seat backrests less bulky and more compliant; rear seat backrest can now be folded forwards and held more or less flat with strap attached to rail below rear seat swab to increase luggage space
		New shape for sun visors – due to increase size/altered shape of windscreen; sun visors can also be swivelled to lie against front side window; sun visors held in position by swivels on windscreen surround (previously held by swivels attached to rear view mirror); rear view mirror larger
		Jack redesigned with two levering points – one to raise, one to lower (previously one levering point); Jack socket 20mm (previously 22mm)
		Windscreen wiper blades longer than previously (larger screen to clear); park to the right (previously to the left)
		Cam now asymmetrical on distributor
		Lockable, chromed push button for engine lid (previously 'T' handle)

Steering wheels

ABOVE: *Late base model steering wheel (from 1967 basic model).*
LEFT: *Early steering wheel with ridges around the rim, before the introduction of the Export model.*

ABOVE: *Standard model steering wheel.*
LEFT: *Export model steering wheel, late 1949–October 1952.*

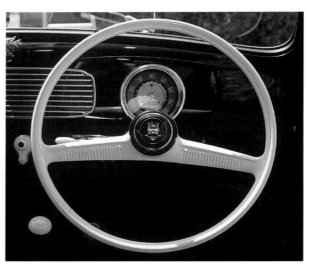

Export model steering wheel, October 1952–August 1955 (early grey-beige, later ivory).

Export model steering wheel, August 1955–July 1959.

The August 1955 design stayed in use when the dash changed in August 1957.

Export steering wheel, August 1959–July 1963.

Export steering wheel, August 1963–July 1965.

1300, 1500 steering wheel, August 1965 onwards.

ABOVE: *The standard steering wheels were made by Petri, which also produced popular accessory versions.*

RIGHT: *Horn button – black with simplified Wolfsburg Crest badge, August 1955–July 1959.*

Date	Chassis no.	Change
		Additional contact surfaces on brake back plate; slots for adjusters and brake cylinder pistons increased in diameter; brake shoes mounted at an angle; box-shaped bearing bracket; drilling in oil trap for fastening (rear brake drums) discontinued and replaced with drainage hole; oil deflector in front of seal – rear wheel bearing
Sep	115 084 567	Warm air hose – diameter 60mm (previously 55mm); heat exchangers – internally ribbed exhaust pipes
Oct	115 161 388	Door-mounted mirror – adhesive backing for mirror
Oct	115 162 922	Clutch release bearing – plastic ring replaces graphite bearing
Oct	115 162 787	Clutch plate splines now phosphate treated; splines of input drive shaft treated with molybdenum disulphide
Oct	115 217 625	Marking ring for adjustment on steering worm
Oct	115 224 816	Wing nut to adjust clutch cable (previously hexagon nut)
Oct	115 247 529	Full synchromesh gearbox on base model – Standard renamed as 1200A by end of the year, but still using 30bhp engine; oil-bath air filter – with crankcase ventilation (07/12/64 115 336 420) (previously none)
Nov	115 255 751	Rocker arm – screw-welded outer oil drilling on valve adjustment (previously open)
Dec	115 349 565	Tension spring for windscreen wiper arms (previously compression spring)
Jan 65	115 460 398	Plastic guide stops on decorative trim moulding for door windows discontinued
Mar	115 579 323	Clutch lining – radial grooves on flywheel side
Mar	115 594 027	Copper core ignition cables, resistor for spark-plug connector; suppressed distributor (previously resistor ignition leads)
Mar	115 623 180	PVC skin on door trim panel reverse
Apr	115 685 587	Straight clutch lever with wing nut for adjusting (previously curved with ball nut for adjusting)
Apr	115 720 690	Valve spring caps with thick walls and defined guide shoulder (previously thin walls and flattened guide shoulder)
May	115 855 772	Heater flap spindle galvanized in heat exchanger
Jun	115 928 504	Base model brought up to date with spring-loaded stays for bonnet (previously single bonnet stay) (Export model received spring-loaded stays '62 model year)
Jun	115 946 462	Rubber sealing for petrol tank cap (previously cork)
July	115 979 202	Last 30bhp engine produced for use in car (*see* below) (industrial use 30bhp engines continued); last 34bhp engine to be fitted to USA spec car – when larger engine appeared, Americans always received the top option

Interior – model dating and identification marks

ABOVE: *Full headlining (cloth until end July 1962), Export model.*

RIGHT: *Small headlining – rest bare painted metal, Standard model.*

FAR RIGHT: *Dashboard-mounted passenger grab handle – fitted as standard on Export model from August 1960.*

Interior light over split panes of rear screen – applicable until October 1952.

From October 1952 the interior light switch was by the left-hand door column – three-way switch from 1954.

1966 – Beetles built between 1 August 1965–31 July 1966

The 1966 model year heralded the arrival of a new 1300 engine and the final disappearance of the old 30bhp engine from the base model's specification, which was now firmly established as the 1200A. Outwardly, the only distinguishing mark of a 1300 was a small badge to that effect on the engine lid. However, a 1966 model can be identified by new flat hubcaps, which replaced the classic dome style.

Date	Chassis no.	Change
2/8/65	116 000 001	1.3ltr 40bhp, 1285cc engine for Deluxe, 1.2ltr 34bhp engine for 1200A – designated FO and DO series respectively; crankshaft from VW 1500 (Type 3) utilized to lengthen the stroke from 64 to 69mm on 1300
		Front axle now ball joint (previously link and king pin)
		Distance between front axle tubes increased from 120mm to 150mm
		Front torsion bars – increased to ten leaves (previously eight)
		Torsion arm link – inner bush metal (previously synthetic)
		Steering stub axle connected to torsion arms by maintenance-free ball joints; eccentric bush on upper joint to allow precise adjustment of camber
		Lubrication nipples in axle tubes – lubrication only required every 10,000km (6,214 miles)
		Shaft of heater control galvanized
		Semi-circular chromed horn ring reintroduced – thumb bars included, but slightly different than previously
		Additional demister vent in top middle of dashboard (Export and Cabriolet)
		Antiquated foot-operated dipswitch replaced by position on stalk on the left-hand side of the steering wheel – also for indicators (Export and Cabriolet); 1200A retains dipswitch
		Backrests of front seats fitted at bottom with a lock to prevent backrest tipping forwards
		Safety locks on doors – safety plate prevents doors swinging open in event of collision
		Door and side trim panels – horizontal brightwork strip
		'New' ventilated steel wheels – a copy of style allocated to VW 1500; slightly better cooling for brakes and lowered overall weight of car; one year only new flat hubcaps – borrowed again from the VW 1500 – domed hubcaps no longer fitted to any model

Heater controls

1949 heater control marked 'H', to left of handbrake.

Rotary heater knob behind handbrake – marked 'H' (central), plus arrows indicating open and close plus letters 'A' and 'Z'.

From 1954 (US models) lettering deleted. From March 1955 also applicable to European models.

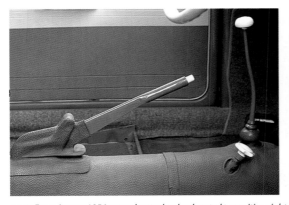

ABOVE: From August 1956 rotary heater knob relocated to position right of and slightly behind the gear knob.

ABOVE MIDDLE: Close-up of rotary heater knob on Standard model around 1960.

RIGHT: 1965 model year onwards there were heater levers with two knobs, instead of one rotary one.

Date	Chassis no.	Change
		1200A – worm and roller steering (previously worm and sector)
		1200A – seat frames redesigned to run on track (previously stud and wing nuts)
		USA-bound models fitted with pull-out hazard warning-light switch below radio-blanking panel and above ignition slot – marked 'emergency 88'
		USA-bound models fitted with gear-shift pattern sticker on dashboard between headlamp and wiper switches
Oct	116 232 227	Wheel-bearing adjustment – slot of clamp nut 2.5mm + 0.5mm (previously 2.0mm – 0.5mm)
Oct	116 240 000	Longer accelerator pump-connecting rod fitted with two holes for cotter pin and spring
Dec	116 460 614	Progressive accelerator pedal with hinged curved plate running on roller attached to cable lever; throttle cable shorter – LHD 2,627mm, RHD 2,535 (previously 2,650 and 2,615mm respectively)
Jan 66	116 471 044	New tapping for thread of oil drain plug on sump plate, with annular ring for seating (previously plate welded in with no annular ring)
Jan	116 463 104	USA models receive new door handles with circular push buttons
		Left-hand heat exchanger – heating pipe one-piece, formerly two pieces welded together
		1200A – carburettor body upper part with bracket for throttle return
Jan	116 478 507	Brass gudgeon pin bush replaced by steel with leaded bronze coat
Apr	116 723 047	Split plastic guide for diaphragm pushrod in fuel pump (previously rubber sleeve); also gasket between cover and diaphragm
May	116 807 190	1200A – for carburettor pre-heating warm air taken from heat exchangers (previously taken from underside of cylinder head)
May	116 809 564	Door handles redesigned, casing of Nirosta steel
May	116 851 572	Steel clutch and brake pedals, previously cast iron
Jun	116 975 949	Pushrods increased in length to 9mm, previously 8.14mm

1967 – Beetles built between 1 August 1966–31 July 1967

For the second year running, the Beetle received a new engine. Beetles bound for the USA and Canada were remarkably different to their European counterparts, although a revised design for the engine lid was common to all.

For a brief period the 1200 Beetle more or less disappeared as an option – even for the home market. A new base model – the 1300A – was fitted with the 40bhp engine, but a 34bhp unit could be specified. However, recession in Germany saw the return of the 1200 in January 1967.

Date	Chassis no.	Change
1/8/66	117 000 001	1.5ltr 44bhp, 1493cc engine for top of the range saloon and, of course, the Cabriolet; H prefix; maximum torque 78lb ft at 2,600rpm offers more usable power across the range
		Preheating of the intake air via two pipes; weighted regulator flap in each intake duct acts as control for intake of pre-heated air
		Disc brakes replace drums on the 1500 Beetle – steering sub-axle altered; 277mm diameter discs, callipers with pistons of 40mm diameter; USA 1500 Beetle retained drums
		Hubs for disc brake models – four wheel bolts, M14 × 1.5 – tightening torque 13m/kg – hole PCD 130mm
		Hubcaps for disc brake models changed – still flat but no longer like VW 1500 (Type 3) had been
		Rear track increased – 1,350mm 1500 Beetle, 1,349mm on 1300 (previously 1,250mm)
		Equalizer spring running transversely under rear luggage area, connected to each axle tube by rods and levers, fitted to all models – providing extra help to torsion bars under load
		Rear quarter panels – reinforcement to wheel arches – plus change of shape to accommodate equalizer spring
		Engine lid shape changed to accommodate USA legislation, resulting in number plate sitting almost vertically; additionally, lower section shorter – overall result more space in the engine compartment (note: twin-pronged air filter, *see* above, has no bearing on redesign of lid as has been suggested); sealing plate inside shortened, engine cover plates narrower, wider seal on engine cover
		VW 1500 badge on engine lid on 1500 models
		Narrower chrome trim, secured with plastic clips (except running boards); holes for clips in bodywork also smaller
		Door lock – same key operated ignition and doors (previously separate)
		Water drainage hole with rubber valve in front of chassis fork
		Door locking plate secured with four rather than three screws
		Dashboard switches made of soft plastic with flat-head knobs; finished in black to prevent reflection; pull knob for ashtray deleted, recess added to ease opening process
		Door and side trim panels amended – no trim, armrest can be used to shut door, recessed bright (flat) pull-out handle to open door, car internally locked via slim push-down button set in metalwork close to bottom and back of side window

Cloth upholstery in Standard model – split era.

Plain vinyl seats as fitted in Standard model, later 1950s and 1960s.

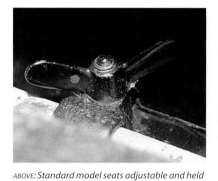

ABOVE: *Standard model seats adjustable and held in position by wing nuts.*

RIGHT: *Cloth upholstery 1950 Export model with bolsters (discontinued November 1951).*

Typical two-tone upholstery of the later 1950s and early 1960s (1958).

Typical piped upholstery of the early 1960s (1963).

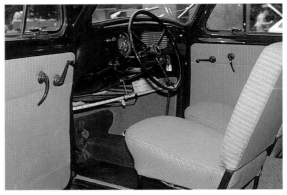

Door cards

Trim varied widely according to the market in the split and oval years. The following are intended to represent general trends:

Door card split, Standard model.

LEFT: *Door card oval, Standard model.*
BELOW: *Door card Export, late 1950s.*

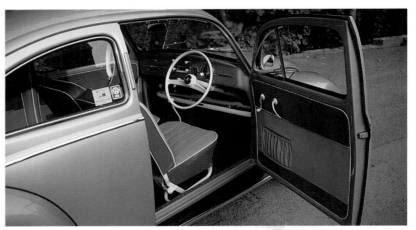

Door card split, Export model.

ABOVE: *Door card oval, Export model.*
RIGHT: *Door card Export, early 1960s.*

Door card 1200 – 1967 (1300, 1500 same but furniture more elaborate).

Door card and interior 1965.

ABOVE: Window winder, circa 1949; Export model chromed with ivory knob; Standard home market painted with black knob.

RIGHT: From 1951, knob had two engraved circles; chromed on Export version.

ABOVE: From 1951, knob had two engraved circles; painted on Standard version.

RIGHT: Door furniture – October 1952–July 1955, Standard model (body colour not applicable).

Door furniture on a Standard model for export – hence chrome with black fittings.

Flat handle for door lock introduced in August 1966.

Window winder from August 1955 – smaller than previously and without groove/rib.

The pre-October 1952 rear seat ashtray was round (pre-June 1950 ashtray was an additional cost option).

Post-October 1952 rear seat ashtray.

specification detail changes month by month

Date	Chassis no.	Change
		Base model – steering wheel now two-spoke with deep-set hub (previously three-spoke) (not to be confused with two-spoke wheel on 1500 and so on – horn on centre button, no semi-circular horn ring, Wolfsburg Crest)
		Indicator switch and horn button new design (Base model)
		Flywheel and transmission casing altered on starter, resulting in smaller pinion diameter
		Steering ignition lock now tongue lock, so lock barrel can be pushed in – single key system (previously pin lock) – ignition key separate
		Fuse box ten fuses, previously eight
		Modified distributor – ignition coil with three connections to terminal 15 (previously two connections)
		Brake lights – bulb sockets modified
		Two-speed wipers connected to rotary switch (previously pull-out) (Base model – single-speed)
		US/Canadian Beetles only: 12V electrics; vertically set sealed beam headlamps; side light (parking light) housed in indicator light (previously within headlamp assembly); shape of wing changed to accommodate vertical headlight (12V sticker on left front door pillar); reversing lamps – separate units, chromed and mounted on the rear bumper; word Volkswagen appears as script on engine compartment lid (previously 1300 and note term 1500 not used); standard seat belts with racing-type buckle secured to a ring mounted between the front seats
Aug	117 050 500	Bowden cable secured with a clip – fuel gauge
Aug	117 054 916	Piston with annular groove oil-pressure relief valve (previously without groove)
Sep	117 197 986	Crankcase studs – sealing rings between crankcase halves (previously self-sealing nuts)
Sep	117 112 756	Steering track rod outer end secured with damping sleeve, inner end with control nut; both intermediate locking plate and rod discontinued
Oct	117 199 633	6V ignition coil – 1500 Beetle – two spade terminals at terminal 15 (previously one connector)
Oct	117 207 566	12V ignition coil – 1500 Beetle – two spade terminals at terminal 15 (previously one connector)
Nov	117 349 409	1500 model – brake fluid reservoir now positioned higher by 17mm
Nov	117 359 672	Oil pipe seamless (previously welded)
Dec	117 374 455	Radius of the bearing surface of stud of the big end cap 2.5mm radius (previously 4mm)
Dec	117 398 501	Hubcaps – shape changed to match 1500
Dec	117 425 908	Front backrest lock now operated from pull-up knob with flat top in upper part of backrest
Jan 67	117 470 115	Some boot lid handles now produced in aluminium (previously all Nirosta)
Jan	117 493 539	Stop collar on bearing three on camshaft increased in size, now 36.2mm (previously 34mm diameter)
Jan	117 496 034	Oil reservoir on door hinges
Apr	117 632 001	Wheel bearing cap with opening for speedometer drive spindle – sealing paint discontinued, now sealed with red metal cement
Apr	117 666 265	Adjustable pushrod for brake master cylinder
		LHD cars – clutch pedal depression limited by stop behind pedal pad
Apr	117 674 559	30 PICT carburettor – upper part fitted with thicker throttle valve spindle and two shims
Jun	117 810 605	Clutch with 1300 engine – 180mm diameter, torsion sprung clutch disc
Jun	117 811 587	Crankshaft with 1500 engine – double oilways in an X arrangement (previously single oilway)

Postscript – 1968 model year

Such were the changes to the Beetle's appearance for the 1968 model year that Volkswagen's marketing department felt fully justified in describing their best-selling product as 'new'. Headlamps set vertically, rather than following the natural contours of the car's body, much stronger and almost girder-like bumpers positioned higher on the body of the Beetle, plus both a shortened boot and engine compartment lid, together with redesigned wings both front and rear, encompassed the main changes. The result, although less aesthetically pleasing, was undoubtedly more appropriate for a new generation of would-be purchasers who were happy to overlook the sad fact that by this time the design of the Beetle was already over 30-years old. The demands of US legislation precipitated most of the changes.

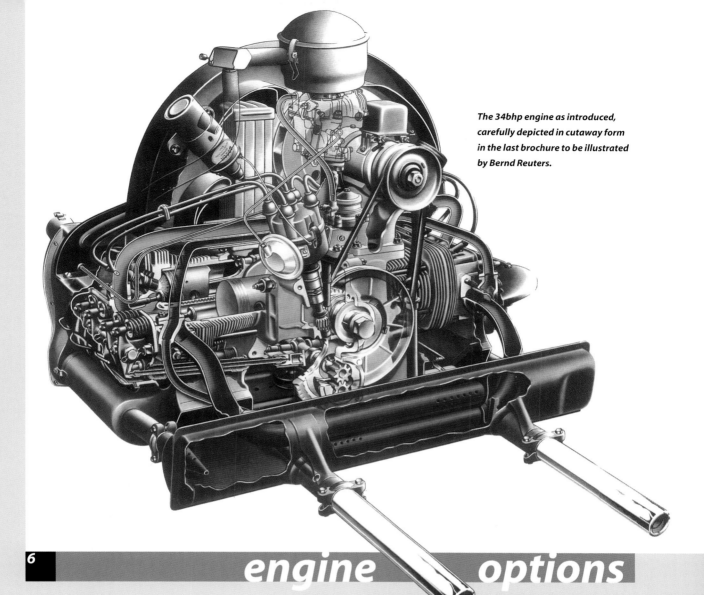

The 34bhp engine as introduced, carefully depicted in cutaway form in the last brochure to be illustrated by Bernd Reuters.

6

engine options

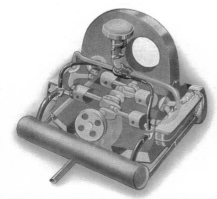

The KdF-Wagen's engine illustrated in the Nazi publication, Der KdF-Wagen von A bis Z, appeared a simple affair. This is the 'original' 985cc engine. Note the exhaust pipe's central position.

INTRODUCTION

Porsche's KdF-Wagen was powered by a 985cc, four-cylinder, air-cooled flat-four engine. With a 70mm bore, 64mm stroke and a compression ratio of 5.8:1, it developed a maximum of 23.5bhp at 3,000rpm. A top speed of 'about 95kph' was quoted in September 1941. March 1943 saw a 1131cc engine fitted to any KdF-Wagens produced. There had been criticism that the KdF-Wagen's engine adopted for use in the military Kübelwagen was underpowered. Further, it didn't comply with the prescribed minimum for any German army vehicle – although for a time this had been conveniently overlooked. The revised engine fitted to both vehicles had a bore of 75mm and maximum power of 25bhp was achieved at 3,300rpm. It was more or less this engine that powered the post-war Beetle until the end of December 1953.

AIR COOLING SYSTEM

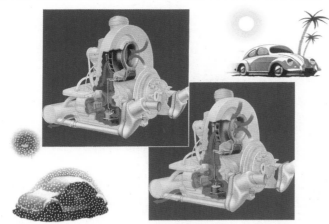

You can drive a Volkswagen for hours at 65 to 70 mph and hardly hear the engine because special sound-proofing keeps out engine noises ● It costs more to build air-cooled engines but we are bearing this extra cost ourselves so that purchasers of Volkswagens may enjoy the advantages of such an engine. You can drive a Volkswagen in the arctic as well as in the tropics, or up the highest mountains without worrying, or leave it out for days in a snowstorm. You can do almost anything with a Volkswagen and still the engine will jump to action at a touch of the starter and purr along contentedly for mile after mile, no matter where you drive it. It will charge up the steepest mountain like a hound on the heels of a jack rabbit. All this is made possible by thermo-matic air cooling. Whether crawling in dense city traffic or dashing up mountains in summer, Volkswagen engines are kept at a proper temperature by automatic thermostatic control which opens or throttles the air stream according to the requirements of the moment. The thermo-matic air cooling system used on Volkswagen engines eliminates 21 sources of trouble inherent to water cooling systems. ● It is in a large part due to the air cooling system that there are so many Volkswagen owners who have driven a quarter of a million kilometers with the same engine and who say they never want any other car than a Volkswagen.

TRANSMISSION

The 4-speed transmission has synchronized second, third and fourth gears. With a flick of the gear-shift lever you have the advantages of fluid drive without the disadvantages. In first gear the Volkswagen can climb a 37% grade. There is not a road anywhere that steep. Fourth speed is built in as top gear on all models and there is no extra charge for it. The Volkswagen transmission is master of any situation that may arise in town or country driving.

CARBURETOR

This is the most advanced type of downdraft carburetor made. It is equipped with an accelerator pump and makes it possible for the engine to give such high performance. It is thanks to this carburetor that the Volkswagen engine springs to action summer and winter at a touch of the starter. It is this carburetor, too, that gives such fast acceleration and such smooth transition. It mixes air and fuel so thoroughly and doses the mixture so precisely that Volkswagens consume very little fuel and yet give remarkably high performance.

Air-cooling explained – with the 25bhp engine.

The 25bhp engine – note the lack of sound-deadening insulation in the engine compartment.

1100 – 25bhp: 1945–53

Volkswagen described the Beetle's engine thus in late 1952:

Design: four-cylinder, four-cycle engine in rear of car
Arrangement of cylinders: horizontally opposed
Bore: 2.953in (75mm)
Stroke: 2.520in (64mm)
Capacity: 69.014cu in (1131cc)
Compression ratio: 5.8:1
VALVES:
Maximum brake horsepower: 25hp at 3,300rpm
Continuous brake hp rating: 24hp at 3,000rpm
Piston speed: 1,263ft/min at 3,000rpm – 6.4m/sec
Oil capacity: 4.4pt (2.5ltr)
Carburettor: downdraft type Solex 28PCI with accelerator pump*
Cooling system: air-cooling by fan, automatically regulated by thermostat
Battery: 6V 70amp/hr
Starter: solenoid type (Bosch EED 0.4/6 L4)
Generator: Bosch RED K 130/6 – 2600 A1 16, with voltage regulator

* Engines manufactured before October 1952 were fitted with a Solex 26VFI or VFJ, HUF to March 1950, followed by a 26 VFIS.

1200 – 30bhp: 1954–60 (Deluxe) and 1965 (Standard/1200A)

With effect from 21 December 1953, the Beetle's engine capacity was increased to 1192cc and performance to 30bhp. Although the stroke remained the same, bore was increased from 75mm to 77mm. The inlet valves – four in number – were increased in diameter from 28.6mm to 30mm to improve breathing, while the distributor benefited from a vacuum advance mechanism. Together with an increased compression ratio – initially raised from 5.8:1 to 6.1:1 – the net effect was an increase in the top speed from 102km/h (63mph) to 110km/h (68mph).

In early 1954, Volkswagen described the Beetle's engine thus:

Design: four-cylinder, four-cycle, ohv type
Arrangement of cylinders: horizontally opposed
Bore: 3.031in (77mm)
Stroke: 2.520in (64mm)
Capacity: 72.740cu in (1192cc)
Compression ratio: 6.1:1*
Maximum brake horsepower: 30hp at 3,400rpm
(*Maximum SAE horsepower:* 36hp at 3,700rpm)

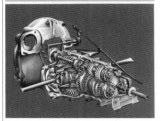

Engine and Transmission

ENGINE The celebrated Volkswagen engine has proved itself three million times over. It is an air-cooled, four-cylinder, four-cycle o.h.v. power plant; mounted at the rear, it is flanged to the transmission housing, which in turn is isolated from the car. Two pairs of cylinders each lie horizontally opposed, giving a low center of gravity and the most efficient use of space. As a typical short-stroke motor it has unusually low piston speeds; this also explains its amazingly low wear, its unflagging endurance on turnpikes, and its proverbial long life. The crankshaft of the engine has four bearings, and is drop-forged of manganese steel, dynamically balanced, and hardened at the bearings. The connecting rods have lead-bronze crankshaft bearings. Engine, transmission, differential, and rear axle form an integral unit, with the result that substantial space and weight are saved, and the engine is conveniently accessible. A Solex down-draft carburetor with booster pump assures smooth transitions, vigorous acceleration, low consumption, and great flexibility. Even at the lowest temperatures the engine always leaps quickly into life; the choke is linked to the butterfly valve to give graded idling. No breaking in is needed with a Volkswagen engine. From the first mile you can safely run it as fast as it will go.

AIR COOLING Air does not freeze, air does not boil. It is the air-cooled engine that makes the Volkswagen ideal for extreme conditions . . . from arctic cold to tropical heat. The engine soon warms up to its best operating temperature, and there is no over-cooling in cold weather. Here is why: the VW air cooling system is linked to the speed of the engine: it works harder as rpm increase. Thermostatic control automatically checks or releases the mass of air drawn in by the blower. At top speed of 68 mph (3400 revolutions), 18 cubic feet of air whip through the Volkswagen engine every second.

COOLED OIL The oil cooler — usually only found in expensive sports cars — contributes to the trouble-free operation of the engine at all temperatures — even under maximum stress. The crankcase capacity of the engine is only 5 pints and the oil is in constant circulation. This oil is pumped as many as 5 times a minute through the oil cooler, which is located at the side of the fan right in the blast of cooling air. When the oil is cold, however, it is automatically carried direct to the lubrication points, by-passing the oil cooler.

TRANSMISSION Rugged construction and positive feel are also found in the synchromesh transmission — so smoothly engineered a woman can handle it with powder-puff ease. The gear ratios are so ideally chosen that maximum performance and economy are guaranteed under all conditions. This transmission is one of the reasons for the superb performance of Volkswagens even on snow and sand, mud and ice.

ABOVE: 30bhp engine.

BELOW: The firm of Okrasa was one of the first to tune the Beetle engine. Ranging from replacement heads with twin inlet ports and larger valves, coupled to a pair of Solex 32PBI carburettors, to more extensive modifications involving a forged longer stroke crankshaft gave a significant gain in performance terms. With a capacity of 1293cc, the engine developed 48bhp.

ABOVE: The 30bhp engine (and gearbox) taken from the 'Engine and Transmission' page of a 1959 model-year brochure.

Oil capacity: 4.4pt (2.5ltr)
Carburettor: downdraft type Solex 28PCI with accelerator pump
Cooling system: air-cooling by fan, automatically regulated by thermostat
Battery: 6V 70amp/hr
Starter: solenoid type (Bosch)
Generator: Bosch 160W with voltage regulator
* The compression ratio was increased from 6.1:1 to 6.6:1 in August 1954.

1200 – 34bhp: 1960–67 and beyond

With effect from August 1960 – for the 1961 model year – the Beetle was upgraded with an engine that resembled the unit fitted to the Transporter from May 1959. Modifications compared to the old 30bhp engine – still an integral part of the Standard model's make-up – included a more robust crankcase, a stronger crankshaft, a removable dynamo pedestal, a modified fuel pump drive and greater spacing of the cylinder barrels. The design of the cylinder head also changed with the use of wedge-shaped combustion chambers, while the valves were positioned at a slant.

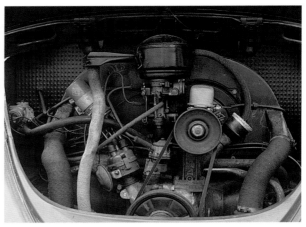

The 34bhp engine without the December 1962 addition of air hoses.

A post December 1962 34bhp engine with air hoses. This unit features the M5 Saxomat 'clutch' – a rarely seen factory-fitted optional extra.

Because the VW is so well made

Take a really close look at the Volkswagen.
Note, just as an example, how the glove compartment is finished. Inside. And if you removed all the trim and upholstery from a VW, you would still find the car completely painted, inside and out.
Is every car made this way? Well, every Volkswagen is. The Volkswagen factory manufactures 3,600 of the VW 1200 models every day. At each stage of production, they are thoroughly checked and tested by senior craftsmen, in fact, 3,700 of them.

There are more inspectors than cars produced per day. As in every factory, we conscientiously test the engine, gear box, brakes, and all other vital units.
In our factory, however, we also pay special attention to the other less vital parts, merely to satisfy our quest for quality. The paint, interior finish, and chrome receive equally painstaking care, making them last for many years, giving you more for your money.
The Volkswagen's body and its flat platform chassis are joined to create a single unit. They are sealed with rubber.

The 34bhp engine and gearbox in cutaway form shown from above, as included in a 1963 brochure.

It has an air-cooled rear engine.

You already know that the engine is air-cooled. But – it's at the rear. Does it matter a jot where the VW engine is? At the front or at the rear?

Well, it does matter to us.

At the rear it's directly above the drive wheels with all its weight on them.

The result: easier to move off when you start. Easier

hill climbing. Easier to drive on sand and through mud.

But better road grip is not the only advantage of having the VW engine at the rear.

It needs no prop-shaft. (The engine's power is transmitted direct to the drive wheels.) Nor does it need a long exhaust pipe.

The undersurface of the car is completely smooth.

It consists of a single metal platform which protects the car against flying stones, snow, sand and water.

And how are the fuel lines and cables protected? They are housed in the strong central steel frame tunnel in the floor.

The result: Nothing can be damaged. Nothing can be torn off.

From a brochure dating from 1965, this cutaway representation of the 34bhp engine was accompanied by text praising its longevity and promoting its robust nature.

A larger dynamo pulley and a smaller crankshaft pulley resulted in a reduction of the speed of the cooling fan and consequently lower noise levels.

Although bore and stroke – at 77mm and 64mm respectively – remained identical to the older 30bhp unit, as did the cubic capacity of 1192cc, the new engine, with a raised compression ratio of 7.0:1 (previously 6.6:1) showed a significant increase in usable power from its extra four horses.

A new Solex carburettor – 28PICT with automatic choke – was installed, although in November 1963 a Solex 28PICT/1 replaced it. This carburettor remained in use until July 1970, some three years past the end of the period covered by this volume.

The visual appearance of the 34bhp engine was altered in December 1962 when the Beetle's heating system was amended to use heat exchangers. As a result, two thick pipes appeared to the right and the left of the engine.

In the last months of 1960 and the first of the following year, Volkswagen described the Beetle's engine as follows:

Design: four-cylinder, four-cycle, ohv type
Arrangement of cylinders: horizontally opposed
Bore: 3.031in (77mm)
Stroke: 2.520in (64mm)
Capacity: 72.74cu in (1192cc)
Compression ratio: 7.0:1
Maximum brake horsepower: 34hp at 3,600rpm
(*Maximum SAE horsepower:* 40hp at 3,900rpm)
Oil capacity: 4.4pt (2.5ltr)
Carburettor: downdraft type Solex 28PICT
with automatic choke and acceleration
pump*
Cooling system: air-cooling by fan,
automatically regulated by thermostat
Battery: 6V 66amp/hr
Starter: solenoid type
Generator: 180W with voltage control

* Engines manufactured after November 1963 were fitted with a Solex 28PICT/1 carburettor.

1300 – 40bhp: 1965–67 and beyond

For the 1966 model year, introduced in August 1965, Volkswagen added a 1300 engine at the top of its Beetle range, thus being available for the Deluxe and the Cabriolet. Although not a new design, the engine offered an extra 6bhp, which was achieved through adoption of the crankshaft from the VW 1500 (Type 3) to lengthen

the stroke from 64mm to 69mm and give an overall capacity of 1285cc. The compression ratio was also increased from the 1200's 7.0:1 to 7.3:1. The net result was an overall increase in power of some 17.5 per cent. Despite the fact that the 'new' engine might have lagged a little when compared to some of its contemporaries, Volkswagen resisted the temptation to introduce twin-port inlets, preferring to ensure that with single-port inlets it remained understressed.

1300 badge on the engine lid – the car's only real distinguishing feature.

Volkswagen chose to describe their 1300 as follows in August 1965:

Design: four-cylinder, four-stroke, rear engine
Arrangement of cylinders: horizontally opposed
Bore: 77mm (3.03in)
Stroke: 69mm (2.72in)
Capacity: 1285cc (78.4cu in)
Compression ratio: 7.3:1
Maximum brake horsepower: 40hp at 4,000rpm
(Maximum SAE horsepower: 50hp at 4,600rpm)
Oil capacity: 4.4pt (2.5ltr)
Carburettor: Solex 30PICT1 downdraft with automatic choke and acceleration pump (from October 1965)
Cooling system: air cooling by fan, automatically regulated by thermostat
Battery: 6V 66amp/hr
Starter: solenoid type

The 1285cc engine – introduced for the 1966 model year.

1500 – 44bhp: 1966–70

Just twelve months after introducing the 1300 engine, Volkswagen added a 1500 unit at the top of the range, which quickly became known as a real driver's engine. Although the 1493cc single-port engine produced just 4bhp more than the 1300, it offered a notable increase in power right across its range. While the 1500's stroke remained the same as the 1300's at 69mm, the bore was enlarged to 83mm. The compression ratio was increased again, this time to 7.5:1. Maximum torque of 78lb ft occurred at 2,600rpm, while the Beetle's top speed was now 125km/h (78mph). Just as a 1300 could be distinguished by an 'F' in front of the number stamped on the crankcase above the dynamo pedestal, so too could the 1500, with all such engine numbers being prefixed by the letter 'H'. These engines can also be distinguished by a twin-pronged air filter – a necessary modification thanks to the intake pre-heating air being taken from both cylinder heads, through two narrow flexible hoses to its destination.

Volkswagen's description of the 1500 engine was as follows in August 1966:

Design: four-cylinder, four-stroke rear engine
Arrangement of cylinders: horizontally opposed
Bore: 83mm (3.27in)
Stroke: 69mm (2.72in)
Capacity: 1493cc (91.10cu in)
Compression ratio: 7.5:1
Maximum brake horsepower: 44hp at 4,000rpm
(Maximum SAE horsepower: 53hp at 4,200rpm)
Oil capacity: 4.4pt (2.5ltr)
Carburettor: downdraft – Solex 30 PICT1 with automatic choke, accelerator pump and oil-bath air cleaner, automatic pre-heating of intake air and mixture
Cooling system: air cooling by fan, automatically regulated by thermostat
Battery: 6V 66amp/hr
Starter: solenoid type

44bhp engine – note the twin air intakes on the oil-bath air-cleaner.

1500 badge – the symbol of the best Beetle engine.

7 *factory-fitted* optional equipment

ABOVE: The service booklet included with Volkswagens purchased in 1962.
RIGHT: Instruction manual cover – 1957–60.

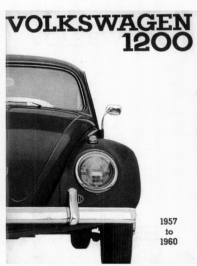

VOLKSWAGEN 1200

1957
to
1960

In order to cater for the demands of individual customers in Germany and more so in certain markets across the world, Beetles were supplied from Wolfsburg and other plants with a large variety of factory-fitted options. Additionally, some options were fitted in order that the Beetle complied with the rules and regulations pertinent to the market to which it was to be exported. In German, the word 'extra' translates as *mehr*, while 'equipment' becomes *ausstattung* – hence the abbreviation used before the numerical designation for a particular extra of 'M'. On occasion, what had previously been optional equipment became either standard or no longer used. In such instances, it was not unusual for an 'M' code to be reallocated to an entirely different option.

The 'M' codes listed here refer to options available on Beetles produced from the earliest days to the end of the 1967 model year. Where applicable, the relevant model/s and country/countries are listed.

'M' code	Description	Years	Model/s	Countries
1	Chrome pack – bumpers, tailpipes, wing-mounted indicators, external handles and so on.	1947–67	Standard	Australia
5	Saxomat semi-automatic transaxle Export 61–67 Standard 65–67	1961–67		not USA
14	'Volkswagen' script badge	1966		
17	Fitting for lap-type seat belts	1962–66		
18	Larger reflectors in brake indicator lights	1962–67	Deluxe	Sweden
19	No headlamp flasher	1966–69	Deluxe	
20	Speedometer indicated in miles	1949		Export
21	Flashing indicators	1955–60		not USA
21	Lockable outside door handles on both sides	1964	Cabriolet	Export
21	Lockable outside door handles on both sides	1964–67	Deluxe & Cabriolet	Export
22	Sealed beam vertical and flash indicators	1955–65	Deluxe & Cabriolet	USA & Canada
22	Sealed beam vertical and flash indicators	1966	Deluxe & Cabriolet	USA & Canada
22	Sealed beam headlamps (angled) with hazard warning-light system	1967		Export – except USA

factory-fitted optional equipment

'M' code	Description	Years	Model/s	Countries
27	Lap-type seat belt – inertia reel	1967		USA & Canada
32	Brake & indicator lights	1956–62		Italy & Australia
34	Special parking lamps – clear lens	1958–65		Italy
34	Clear front indicator lenses – yellow parking lens, backrest lock	1966		Italy
34	Clear front indicator lenses – yellow parking lens	1967		Italy
35	Yellow parking lamp warning light	1958–65		Italy
37	No hazard warning-light system	1966–74		Italy & France
46	Side repeater indicators	1961–74		Israel, Italy, Denmark & Norway
47	Crank starting handle (Standard to 1949)	1947–53		
47	Reversing lights on bumper	1967	Deluxe & Cabriolet	
55	Steering wheel lock with ignition/starter switch	1967–69		all export markets – Standard in Germany
60	Eberspacher auxiliary heater	1955		
62	Washer reservoir with reduced air space, additional external rear-view mirror, convex, on right	1961–70		Sweden
67	Larger 6V 77Ah battery and cover (USA to 1966 only)	1956–67	Deluxe & Cabriolet	Export
74	Mudflaps – rear	1956		
82	Side lenses in front indicators	1966–67		Denmark
86	VW 1200, but without compensating spring	1967		
87	Single circuit drums 37bhp engine	1967		Not USA
87	Single circuit drums 40bhp engine	1967		Not USA
88	Single circuit drums 34bhp	1967		Not USA
89	Laminated windscreen	1950		
93	Opening rear side windows (not available on Standard model until 1965)	1952		
94	Lockable engine-lid cover	1949		
102	Heated rear window (6V)	1965–67		
103	Reinforced bumpers	1952		
105	Harder rubber/metal bearings for transmission mountings	1961		
106	Special cloth upholstery	1952	Standard & Deluxe	West German Police & Post Office
107	Bumpers with overriders (towel-rail style) Initially for US market – introduced 1955)	1956–67		
110	Synchromesh gears, hydraulic brakes, also trim strips	1962	Standard	Canada
110	Full synchromesh, trim strips, but without external mirror	1962–66	Standard	Canada
110	With M 129, trim strips, PVC-lined luggage space, but without external mirror	1967	Standard	Canada
123	Special remote interference suppression	1961		France
124	Yellow lens headlamps	1956		France
129	34bhp engine	1967	Standard	
137	Dual circuit drum brakes	1967	Deluxe & Cabriolet	Export markets
139	Sealed beam headlamp assemblies	1952–66		Export
139	Dual circuit drum brakes	1967–69	Standard	Canada & Scandinavia
148	Primary coat head and tail lamp bezels	1952–66		
153	Oil-bath air cleaner and cyclone filter	1961–65		
153	Double oil-bath air-filter system	1966		
158	Door hinge mirror and hinge pin lid – LHD	1961–67	Deluxe & Cabriolet	
167	12V 88Ah battery	1967	Deluxe & Cabriolet	USA
179	Locking device for front seat backrest	1967	Standard	
218	Wheel trim rings	1954–69	Cabriolet	
218	Wheel trim rings	1967–69	Deluxe	
232	Lockable tonneau cover	1949	Cabriolet	
240	Engine with dished pistons for lower octane fuel – E on 37bhp 1300 engine and L on 40bhp 1500 engine	1966–70		
610	12V electrical system	1958–67		
992	Electric clock	1958–61	Cabriolet	

Part of the paint line-up for 1966 models.

Top colour chart — 1966 exterior colours:

Außenfarben Exterior colours Couleurs de la carrosserie Colores exteriores Cores dos carros Carrosserie-kleuren	rubinrot ruby red rouge rubis rubi rubi robijnrood	perlweiß pearl white blanc perle blanco perla branco pérola parelwit	seeblau sea blue bleu lac azul lago azul lago zeeblauw	bahamablau Bahama blue bleu Bahama azul Bahama azul Baama bahamablauw	schwarz black noir negro preto zwart	seesand sea sand sable marin arena de playa areia do mar zandgrijs	javagrün Java green vert Java verde Java verde Java javagroen	fontanagrau Fontana grey gris Fontana gris Fontana cinzento Fontana fontanagrijs

Unter jeder Außenfarbe sind die möglichen Kombinationen aufgeführt. Die einzelnen Verdeckfarben und Sitzbezüge finden Sie rechts abgebildet.

The possible combinations are indicated under each exterior colour. The various tonneau cover colours and seat upholstery materials are shown on the right.

Toutes les combinaisons possibles vous sont indiquées au-dessous de chaque couleur de carrosserie. Voici à droite les différentes couleurs de capotes et des garnitures des sièges.

Debajo de cada color exterior se muestran las combinaciones posibles. Se muestran a la derecha los diferentes colores de capota y tapizados para asientos.

Veja as combinações possíveis em baixo de cada cor. A cor dos tejadilhos e dos estofos estão reproduzidos à direita.

Bij elke carrosseriekleur zijn de mogelijke combinaties aangegeven. De afzonderlijke kleuren kapbekleding en stoelbekledingen.

Kunstledersitze bei Limousinen auf Wunsch gegen Mehrpreis. / Leatherette seat upholstery is available on sedans at extra charge. / Sur demande, garnitures des sièges en similicuir sur la conduite intérieure, moyennant supplément. / A petición y con recargo en el precio: asientos de cuero artificial en los Sedans. / Estofos dos assentos em couro artificial, a desejo e contra um pequeno acréscimo no preço, para o Sedan. / Kunstlederen zittingen in limousines op verzoek en tegen bijbetaling.

Beispiel: Bestellnummer . . . 11 10 58
Karosserie rubinrot . . . 11 . . .
Verdeck schwarz . . . 10 .
Sitzbezüge . . . 58

Example: Order No. . . . 11 10 58
Bodywork ruby red . . . 11 . .
Top black . . . 10 .
Seat upholstery material . . . 58

Exemple: Numéro de commande . . . 11 10 58
Carrosserie rouge rubis . . . 11 . .
Capote noire . . . 10 .
Garnitures de sièges . . . 58

Ejemplo: número de pedido . . . 11 10 58
Carrocería rubí . . . 11 . .
Techo negro . . . 10 .
Tapizados para asientos . . . 58

Exemplo: número de encomenda . . . 11 10 58
Carroçaria rubi . . . 11 . .
Tejadilho preto . . . 10 .
Estofos . . . 58

Voorbeeld: bestelnummer . . . 11 10 58
Carrosserie robijnrood . . . 11 . .
Kap zwart . . . 10 .
Stoelbekleding . . . 58

INTRODUCTION

The KdF-Wagen was invariably presented in glossy black paint and this remained an option for the post-war Beetle throughout the period covered by this volume. In the immediate aftermath of the war the majority of the cars produced were painted in grey, blue, or black, while the finish invariably bordered on the matt look, due to the quality of materials available. A typical month's supply of Beetles is indicated in the following chart, which dates from April 1947.

Control number	Released to	Quantity	Colour
Volk 176	F.I.A.T.	45	Black
Volk 168	British Air Force of Occupation	90	Blue
Volk 169	British Army of the Rhine	150	Green
Volk 170	Army Cinema Corp	12	Green
Volk 172	Control Commission	250	Black
Volk 171	NAAFI	12	Blue or Black
Volk 174	American Exchange Service	500	Blue, Black or Grey
Volk 155	Allied Control Authority Austria	50	Blue or Black

During 1948 and the first months of 1949 – before the debut of the Export, or Deluxe, model – a definite improvement in the quality of paint finish can be detected in surviving photographs – particularly for those cars trimmed with a little extra chrome for possible destination over Germany's borders. Apart from the military colours employed, a pattern emerged of supplying Beetles in three colour options. These were Pearl Grey (L21), Black (L41) and Dark Blue (L32). With the arrival of the Export/Deluxe model the system soon settled down into a regular pattern of paint options, which included the occasional alternative exclusive to the Standard model. Later still, a practice emerged of either sharing, or in one instance demoting, a colour from use on the Export model to become an option on the Standard. Likewise, the top-of-the-range Cabriolet benefited from some exclusive paint options and on occasion trims.

1949: before the introduction of the Export Model		
Body colour	**Wheel hub & rim colour**	**Optional wheel & rim colour**
L11 Pastel Green	L11 Pastel Green	L41 Black
L13 Medium Green	L13 Medium Green	L41 Black
L14 Reseda Green	L14 Reseda Green	L41 Black
L21 Pearl Grey	L21 Pearl Grey	L23 Silver Grey
L23 Silver Grey	L23 Silver Grey	L21 Pearl Grey
L32 Dark Blue	L32 Dark Blue	L41 Black
L41 Black	L41 Black	L50 Coral Red
L51 Bordeaux Red	L51 Bordeaux Red	L50 Coral Red

Pearl Grey L21, 1948–March 1953.

EXPORT/DELUXE AND STANDARD/1200A PAINT OPTIONS: 1949 TO 1967

1949: from July 1949 and the introduction of the Export Model (July 1949–May 1950)

Body colour	Wheel hub & rim colour	Wheel hub pinstripe Colour (Export Only)
L11 Pastel Green	L11 Pastel Green	L41 Black
L13 Medium Green	L13 Medium Green	L60 Ivory
L14 Reseda Green	L14 Reseda Green	L41 Black
L21 Pearl Grey*	L21 Pearl Grey	L41 Black
L23 Silver Grey	L23 Silver Grey	L41 Black
L32 Dark Blue	L32 Dark Blue	L60 Ivory
L41 Black*	L41 Black	L50 Black
L50 Coral Red	L50 Coral Red	L41 Black
L51 Bordeaux Red	L51 Bordeaux Red	L60 Ivory
L70 Medium Brown	L70 Medium Brown	L60 Ivory

(*Standard Model)

Pastel Green L11, 1949–December 1953.

1950

Body colour	Wheel hub & rim colour	Wheel hub pinstripe Colour (Export Only)	Sunroof external colour
L11 Pastel Green	L11 Pastel Green	L41 Black	11 Pastel Green
L13 Medium Green	L13 Medium Green	L60 Ivory	13 Medium Green
L14 Reseda Green	L14 Reseda Green	L41 Black	14 Reseda Green
L21 Pearl Grey*	L21 Pearl Grey		21 Pearl Grey
L23 Silver Grey	L23 Silver Grey	L41 Black	23 Silver Grey
L32 Dark Blue*	L32 Dark Blue	L60 Ivory	32 Dark Blue
L41 Black	L41 Black	L60 Ivory	41 Black
L50 Coral Red	L50 Coral Red	L41 Black	50 Coral Red
L51 Bordeaux Red	L51 Bordeaux Red	L60 Ivory	51 Bordeaux Red
L70 Medium Brown	L70 Medium Brown	L60 Ivory	70 Medium Brown
L76 Brown Beige	L76 Brown Beige	L60 Ivory	76 Brown Beige
L87 Pearl White	L87 Pearl White	L41 Black	87 Pearl White

(*Standard Model)

1951

Body colour	Wheel rim colour	Export hub colour	Sunroof external colour
L11 Pastel Green	L11 Pastel Green	L75 Light Beige	11 Pastel Green
L13 Medium Green	L13 Medium Green	L75 Light Beige	13 Medium Green
L14 Reseda Green	L14 Reseda Green	L75 Light Beige	14 Reseda Green
L21 Pearl Grey*	L21 Pearl Grey		21 Pearl Grey
L23 Silver Grey	L23 Silver Grey	L75 Light Beige	23 Silver Grey
L31 Dove Blue	L31 Dove Blue	L75 Light Beige	31 Dove Blue
L32 Dark Blue*	L32 Dark Blue	L75 Light Beige	32 Dark Blue
L36 Azure Blue	L36 Azure Blue	L75 Light Beige	36 Azure Blue
L37 Medium Blue*	L37 Medium Blue	L75 Light Beige	37 Medium Blue
L41 Black	L41 Black	L75 Light Beige	41 Black
L55 Maroon Red	L55 Maroon Red	L75 Light Beige	55 Maroon Red
L70 Medium Brown	L70 Medium Brown	L75 Light Beige	70 Medium Brown
L73 Chestnut Brown	L73 Chestnut Brown	L75 Light Beige	73 Chestnut Brown
L87 Pearl White	L87 Pearl White	L53 Sealing Wax Red	87 Pearl White
L90 Sand Beige	L90 Sand Beige	L53 Sealing Wax Red	90 Sand Beige

(*Standard Model)

Dove Blue L31, 1951–September 1952.

1952 (to end of September)

Body colour	Wheel rim colour	Export hub colour	Sunroof external colour
L11 Pastel Green	L11 Pastel Green	L75 Light Beige	11 Pastel Green
L13 Medium Green	L13 Medium Green	L75 Light Beige	13 Medium Green
L14 Reseda Green	L14 Reseda Green	L75 Light Beige	14 Reseda Green
L21 Pearl Grey	L21 Pearl Grey		21 Pearl Grey
L23 Silver Grey	L23 Silver Grey	L75 Light Beige	23 Silver Grey
L31 Dove Blue	L31 Dove Blue	L75 Light Beige	31 Dove Blue
L32 Dark Blue*	L32 Dark Blue	L75 Light Beige	32 Dark Blue
L36 Azure Blue	L36 Azure Blue	L75 Light Beige	36 Azure Blue
L37 Middle Blue*	L37 Medium Blue	L75 Light Beige	37 Middle Blue
L41 Black	L41 Black	L75 Light Beige	41 Black
L55 Maroon Red	L55 Maroon Red	L75 Light Beige	55 Maroon Red
L70 Medium Brown	L70 Medium Brown	L75 Light Beige	70 Medium Brown
L73 Chestnut Brown	L73 Chestnut Brown	L75 Light Beige	73 Chestnut Brown
L87 Pearl White	L87 Pearl White	L53 Sealing Wax Red	87 Pearl White
L90 Sand Beige*	L90 Sand Beige	L53 Sealing Wax Red	90 Sand Beige

(*Standard Model)

Medium Blue L37, 1951–July 1958.

1952–53 (October 1952–March 1953)

Body colour	Wheel rim colour	Export hub colour	Sunroof external colour
L11 Pastel Green	L11 Pastel Green	L87 Pearl White	11 Pastel Green
L13 Medium Green*	L13 Medium Green	L87 Pearl White	13 Medium Green
L21 Pearl Grey*	L21 Pearl Grey	L87 Pearl White	21 Pearl Grey
L36 Azure Blue	L36 Azure Blue	L87 Pearl White	36 Azure Blue
L37 Middle Blue*	L37 Medium Blue	L87 Pearl White	37 Middle Blue
L41 Black	L41 Black	L87 Pearl White	41 Black
L55 Maroon Red	L55 Maroon Red	L87 Pearl White	55 Maroon Red
L70 Medium Brown	L70 Medium Brown	L87 Pearl White	70 Medium Brown
L73 Chestnut Brown	L73 Chestnut Brown	L87 Pearl White	73 Chestnut Brown
L90 Sand Beige*	L90 Sand Beige	L53 Sealing Wax Red	90 Sand Beige

(*Standard Model)

1953 (March–December 1953)

Body colour	Wheel rim colour	Export hub colour	Sunroof external colour
L11 Pastel Green	L11 Pastel Green	L87 Pearl White	11 Pastel Green
L19 Atlantic Green	L19 Atlantic Green	L87 Pearl White	19 Atlantic Green
L35 Metallic Blue	L35 Metallic Blue	L87 Pearl White	35 Metallic Blue
L37 Middle Blue*	L37 Medium Blue	L87 Pearl White	37 Middle Blue
L41 Black	L41 Black	L87 Pearl White	41 Black
L73 Chestnut Brown	L73 Chestnut Brown	L87 Pearl White	73 Chestnut Brown
L225 Jupiter Grey*	L225 Jupiter Grey	L87 Pearl White	225 Jupiter Grey
L271 Texas Brown	L271 Texas Brown	L87 Pearl White	271 Texas Brown
L272 Sahara Beige	L272 Sahara Beige	L53 Sealing Wax Red	272 Sahara Beige

(*Standard Model)

BELOW LEFT: *Metallic Blue L35, March 1953–December 1953.*

BELOW MIDDLE: *Jupiter Grey L225, March 1953–July 1963.*

BELOW RIGHT: *Texas Brown L271, March 1953–March 1955.*

1954 (January 1954–February 1955)

Body colour	Wheel rim colour	Export hub colour	Sunroof external colour
L37 Middle Blue*	L37 Medium Blue	L87 Pearl White	37 Middle Blue
L41 Black	L41 Black	L87 Pearl White	550 Black
L213 Iceland Green	L213 Iceland Green	L87 Pearl White	568 Iceland Green
L225 Jupiter Grey*	L225 Jupiter Grey	L225 Jupiter Grey	225 Jupiter Grey
L227 Strato Silver	L227 Strato Silver	L82 Silver White	567 Strato Silver
L271 Texas Brown	L271 Texas Brown	L87 Pearl White	560 Texas Brown
L275 Light Beige	L275 Light Beige	L87 Pearl White	569 Light Beige
L276 Ultramaroon	L276 Ultramaroon	L87 Pearl White	570 Ultramaroon

(*Standard Model option)

1955 (March 1955–March 1956)

Body colour	Wheel rim colour	Export hub colour	Sunroof external colour
L37 Middle Blue*	L37 Medium Blue	L87 Pearl White	37 Middle Blue
L41 Black	L41 Black	L87 Pearl White	550 Black
		L328 Steel Grey**	
L225 Jupiter Grey*	L225 Jupiter Grey	L225 Jupiter Grey	225 Jupiter Grey
L227 Strato Silver	L227 Strato Silver	L82 Silver White	567 Strato Silver
L313 Reed Green	L313 Reed Green	L87 Pearl White	577 Reed Green
L315 Jungle Green	L315 Jungle Green	L83 White Green	578 Jungle Green
L324 Polar Silver	L324 Polar Silver	L87 Pearl White	576 Polar Silver
L370 Nile Beige	L370 Nile Beige	L277 Silver Beige	575 Nile Beige

(*Standard Model)

(** From August 1955)

Jungle Green L315, March 1955–March 1956.

1956 and 1957 model year (April 1956–July 1957)

Body colour	Wheel rim colour	Hub colour	Sunroof external colour
L37 Middle Blue*	L37 Medium Blue	L87 Pearl White	37 Middle Blue
L41 Black	L41 Black	L81 Parchment White	550 Black
L225 Jupiter Grey*	L225 Jupiter Grey	L225 Jupiter Grey	225 Jupiter Grey
L240 Agave Green	L247 Pine Green	L87 Pearl White	584 Agave Green
L324 Polar Silver	L328 Steel Grey	L87 Pearl White	576 Polar Silver
L331 Horizon Blue	L33 Greyish Blue	L82 Silver White	582 Horizon Blue
L351 Coral Red	L74 Rusty Brown	L277 Silver Beige	581 Coral Red
L378 Prairie Beige	L77 Dark Beige	L277 Silver Beige	579 Prairie Beige
L412 Diamond Green	L211 Blue Green	L277 Silver Beige	580 Diamond Green

(*Standard Model)

Horizon Blue L331, April 1956–July 1957.

1958 model year (August 1957–July 1958)

Body colour	Wheel rim colour	Hub colour	Sunroof external colour
L37 Middle Blue*	L37 Medium Blue	L87 Pearl White	37 Middle Blue
L41 Black	L41 Black	L81 Parchment White	41 Black
L225 Jupiter Grey*	L225 Jupiter Grey	L225 Jupiter Grey	225 Jupiter Grey
L240 Agave Green	L247 Pine Green	L87 Pearl White	240 Agave Green
L243 Diamond Grey	L244 Moss Green	L87 Pearl White	243 Diamond Grey
L245 Light Bronze	L256 Grey Green	L87 Pearl White	245 Light Bronze
L334 Glacier Blue	L30 Grey Blue	L82 Silver White	334 Glacier Blue
L335 Capri Blue	L336 Deep Blue	L82 Silver White	335 Capri Blue
L351 Coral Red	L74 Rusty Brown	L277 Silver Beige	581 Coral Red

(*Standard Model)

Diamond Grey L243, August 1957–July 1959.

Agave Green and Coral Red – L240 and L351 – two colour options from the 1958 model-year range.

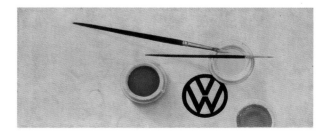

1959 model year (August 1958–July 1959)

Body colour	Wheel rim colour	Hub colour	Sunroof external colour
L14 Mignonette Green	L244 Moss Green	L87 Pearl White	601 Dull Green
L41 Black	L41 Black	L81 Parchment White	550 Black
L225 Jupiter Grey*	L225 Jupiter Grey	L225 Jupiter Grey	225 Jupiter Grey
L243 Diamond Grey	L244 Moss Green	L87 Pearl White	243 Diamond Grey
L335 Capri Blue	L336 Deep Blue	L82 Silver White	335 Capri Blue
L343 Kalahari Beige	L343 Kalahari Beige	L450 Pale Brown	603 Earth Brown
L344 Rush Green*	L344 Rush Green	L344 Rush Green	611 Jade Green
L358 Garnet Red	L359 Ruby Red	L81 Parchment White	602 Garnet Red
L434 Fjord Blue	L30 Grey Blue	L82 Silver White	590 Grey Blue

(*Standard Model)

1960 model year (August 1959–July 1960)

Body colour	Wheel rim colour	Hub colour	Sunroof external colour
L41 Black	L41 Black	L81 Parchment White	550 Black
L225 Jupiter Grey*	L225 Jupiter Grey	L225 Jupiter Grey	225 Jupiter Grey
L344 Rush Green*	L344 Rush Green	L344 Rush Green	611 Jade Green
L346 Mango Green			
L349 Jade Green			
L363 Arctic Blue			
L419 Ceramic Green			
L436 Indigo Blue			
L440 Flint Grey			
L451 Indian Red			

(*Standard Model)

Indian Red L451, August 1959–July 1960.

1961 model year (August 1960–July 1961)

Body colour	Wheel rim colour	Hub colour	Sunroof external colour
L41 Black	L471 Stone Beige	L464 Slate Grey	Black
L87 Pearl White	L87 Pearl White	L479 Clay Beige	Pearl White
L225 Jupiter Grey*	L464 Slate Grey	L392 Misty Grey	Jupiter Grey
L344 Rush Green*	L344 Rush Green	L344 Rush Green	Jade Green
L380 Turquoise	L286 Turquoise White	L381 Sea Green	Turquoise
L390 Gulf Blue	L392 Misty Grey	L393 Kings Blue	Gulf Blue
L391 Pastel Blue	L286 Turquoise White	L394 Night Blue	Pastel Blue
L456 Ruby Red	L471 Stone Beige	L457 Cadmium Red	Ruby Red
L478 Beryl Green	L287 Opal White	L382 Olive Green	Beryl Green

(*Standard Model)

Ruby Red L456, August 1960–July 1967.

RIGHT: *Beryl Green L478, August 1960–July 1963.*
MIDDLE RIGHT: *Turquoise L380, August 1960–July 1963.*
FAR RIGHT: *Pearl White L87, August 1960–July 1967.*

1962 model year (August 1961–July 1962)

Body colour	Wheel rim colour	Hub colour	Sunroof external colour
L41 Black	L471 Stone Beige	L464 Slate Grey	Black
L87 Pearl White	L87 Pearl White	L479 Clay Beige	Pearl White
L225 Jupiter Grey*	L464 Slate Grey	L392 Misty Grey	Jupiter Grey
L344 Rush Green*	L344 Rush Green	L344 Rush Green	Jade Green
L380 Turquoise	L286 Turquoise White	L381 Sea Green	Turquoise
L390 Gulf Blue	L392 Misty Grey	L393 Kings Blue	Gulf Blue
L456 Ruby Red	L471 Stone Beige	L457 Cadmium Red	Ruby Red
L469 Anthracite Grey	L471 Stone Beige	L464 Slate Grey	Anthracite Grey
L478 Beryl Green	L287 Opal White	L382 Olive Green	Beryl Green

(*Standard Model)

paint and trim colours

1963 model year August 1962–July 1963)

Body colour	Wheel rim colour	Export hub colour	Sunroof external colour
L41 Black	L471 Stone Beige	L464 Slate Grey	Black
L87 Pearl White	L87 Pearl White	L479 Clay Beige	Pearl White
L225 Jupiter Grey*	L464 Slate Grey	L392 Misty Grey	Jupiter Grey
L344 Rush Green*	L344 Rush Green	L344 Rush Green	Jade Green
L380 Turquoise	L286 Turquoise White	L381 Sea Green	Turquoise
L390 Gulf Blue**	L392 Misty Grey	L393 Kings Blue	Gulf Blue
L456 Ruby Red	L471 Stone Beige	L457 Cadmium Red	Ruby Red
L469 Anthracite Grey	L471 Stone Beige	L464 Slate Grey	Anthracite Grey
L478 Beryl Green	L287 Opal White	L382 Olive Green	Beryl Green

(*Standard Model)

(**Standard model from February 1963)

1964 model year (August 1963–July 1964)

Body colour	Wheel rim colour	Export hub colour	Sunroof now metal
L41 Black	L87 Pearl White	L41 Black	
L87 Pearl White*	L87 Pearl White	L41 Black	
L360 Sea Blue*	L289 Blue White	L41 Black	
L456 Ruby Red*	L87 Pearl White	L41 Black	
L469 Anthracite Grey*	L87 Pearl White	L41 Black	
L518 Java Green	L87 Pearl White	L41 Black	
L519 Bahama Blue	L289 Blue White	L41 Black	
L572 Panama Beige	L87 Pearl White	L41 Black	

(*Standard Model)

Sea Blue L360, August 1963–July 1966.

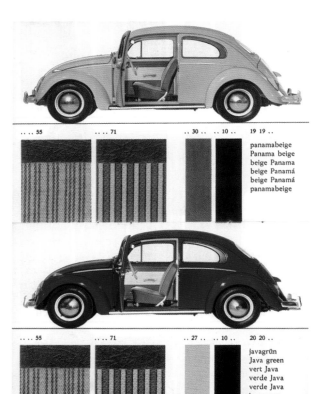

panamabeige
Panama beige
beige Panama
beige Panamá
beige Panamá
panamabeige

javagrün
Java green
vert Java
verde Java
verde Java
javagroen

Java Green L518, August 1963–July 1967.

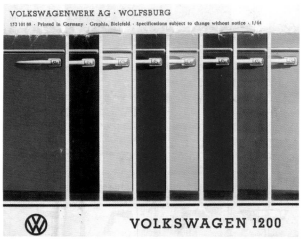

ABOVE: Panama Beige and Java Green circa 1964 – this brochure should have contained a disclaimer that printing processes don't necessarily allow accurate reproduction of all paint colours!

RIGHT: Clever – all the paint options for the '64 model year shown at once, although again colour reproduction leaves a little to be desired!

1965 model year (August 1964–July 1965)

Body colour	Wheel rim colour	Export hub colour
L41 Black	L87 Pearl White	L41 Black
L87 Pearl White*	L87 Pearl White	L41 Black
L360 Sea Blue*	L289 Blue White	L41 Black
L456 Ruby Red*	L87 Pearl White	L41 Black
L518 Java Green	L87 Pearl White	L41 Black
L519 Bahama Blue	L289 Blue White	L41 Black
L572 Panama Beige	L87 Pearl White	L41 Black
L595 Fontana Grey*	L87 Pearl White	L41 Black

(*1200A Option)

Fontana Grey L595, August 1964–July 1967.

1966 model year (August 1965–July 1966)

Body colour	Wheel rim colour	Export hub colour
L41 Black	L87 Pearl White	L41 Black
L87 Pearl White*	L87 Pearl White	L41 Black
L360 Sea Blue*	L289 Blue White	L41 Black
L456 Ruby Red*	L87 Pearl White	L41 Black
L518 Java Green	L87 Pearl White	L41 Black
L519 Bahama Blue	L289 Blue White	L41 Black
L568 Sea Sand	L87 Pearl White	L41 Black
L595 Fontana Grey*	L87 Pearl White	L41 Black

(*1200A Option)

1967 model year (August 1966–July 1967)

Body colour	Wheel rim colour	Export hub colour
L41 Black	L282 Lotus White	LD43 Grey Black
L87 Pearl White**	L282 Lotus White	LD43 Grey Black
L282 Lotus White	L282 Lotus White	LD43 Grey Black
L456 Ruby Red*	L282 Lotus White	LD43 Grey Black
L518 Java Green	L282 Lotus White	LD43 Grey Black
L595 Fontana Grey*	L680 Cumulus White	LD43 Grey Black
L620 Savanna Beige	L282 Lotus White	LD43 Grey Black
L633 VW Blue	L680 Cumulus White	LD43 Grey Black
L639 Zenith Blue	L282 Lotus White	LD43 Grey Black

(*1200A Option)

(** available on 1200A only)

ABOVE: VW Blue L633, August 1966–July 1968.
RIGHT: Zenith Blue L639, August 1966–July 1968.

THE KARMANN CABRIOLET – PAINT AND HOOD COMBINATIONS

More complex than the Saloon, in the early days of Cabriolet production optional side colours could be specified. Likewise, there were choices of hood colour available, and for a time paint options were extended to colours not available for purchasers of the Saloon.

1949

Exterior colour	Optional colours for side panels	Cabriolet hood colour options
L19 Atlantic Green		V1 Black, V3 Green, V21 Beige
L19 Atlantic Green	L11 Pastel Green	V3 Green
L41 Black		V1 Black, V21 Beige
L41 Black	L50 Coral Red,	
L60 Ivory, L71 Beige	V1 Black	
L50 Coral Red		V1 Black
L50 Coral Red	L60 Ivory	V1 Black
L70 Medium Brown	L60 Ivory, L71 Beige	V1 Black, V16 Brown
L71 Beige		V1 Black, V16 Brown

1950

Exterior colour	Optional colours for side panels	Cabriolet hood colour options
L19 Atlantic Green	L11 Pastel Green	V1 Black, V3 Green, V21 Beige
L19 Atlantic Green		V3 Green
L41 Black		V1 Black
L41 Black	L60 Ivory, L71 Beige	V1 Black
L41 Black	L50 Coral Red	V1 Black, V21 Beige
L50 Coral Red		V1 Black
L50 Coral Red	L60 Ivory	V1 Black
L60 Ivory		V1 Black
L70 Medium Brown	L60 Ivory, L71 Beige	V1 Black, V16 Brown
L71 Beige		V1 Black, V16 Brown

1951 and January–September 1952

Exterior colour	Optional colours for side panels	Cabriolet hood colour options
L19 Atlantic Green		V1 Black, V3 Green, V21 Beige,
L19 Atlantic Green	L11 Pastel Green	V3 Green
L31 Dove Blue		V1 Black, V4 Blue, V21 Beige
L31 Dove Blue	L60 Ivory	V4 Blue, V21 Beige, V31 Grey
L31 Dove Blue	L71 Beige	V1 Black V4 Blue, V21 Beige
L41 Black		V1 Black, V21 Beige
L41 Black	L60 Ivory	V1 Black
L41 Black	L71 Beige	V1 Black, V21 Beige
L54 Poppy Red		V1 Black, V21 Beige
L54 Poppy Red	L60 Ivory	V1 Black, V21 Beige
L60 Ivory		V1 Black
L70 Medium Brown		V1 Black, V16 Brown, V21 Beige
L70 Medium Brown	L60 Ivory	V1 Black, V16 Brown
L70 Medium Brown	L71 Beige	V1 Black, V16 Brown, V21 Beige
L71 Beige		V1 Black, V16 Brown
L81 Parchment White		V1 Black

1952–53 (October 1952–March 1953)

Exterior colour	Optional colours for side panels	Cabriolet hood colour options
L19 Atlantic Green	L11 Pastel Green	V1 Black, V3 Green, V21 Beige
L21 Pearl Grey	L23 Silver Grey	V1 Black, V21 Beige, V28 Dark Grey
L36 Azure Blue	L23 Silver Grey	V4 Blue, V21 Beige, V31 Grey
L41 Black		V1 Black, V21 Beige, V31 Grey
L54 Poppy Red		V1 Black, V21 Beige, V28 Dark Grey
L70 Medium Brown	L71 Beige	V1 Black, V21 Beige
L71 Beige		V16 Brown
L81 Parchment White		V1 Black
L90 Sand Beige		V1 Black, V16 Brown

1953 (April–December 1953)

Exterior colour	Optional colours for side panels	Cabriolet hood colour options
L19 Atlantic Green	L11 Pastel Green	V1 Black, V3 Green, V21 Beige
L35 Metallic Blue		V1 Black V21 Beige, V31 Grey
L41 Black		V1 Black, V21 Beige, V31 Grey
L54 Poppy Red		V1 Black, V21 Beige, V31 Grey
L81 Parchment White		V1 Black
L271 Texas Brown	L272 Sahara Beige	V1 Black, V16 Brown, V21 Beige
L272 Sahara Beige		V1 Black V16 Brown

1954 (January 1954–February 1955)

Exterior colour	Cabriolet hood colour options
L41 Black	V1 Black, V21 Beige, V31 Grey
L54 Poppy Red	V1 Black, V21 Beige, V31 Grey
L81 Parchment White	V1 Black
L210 Beige Green	V1 Black, V3 Green, V31 Grey
L219 Congo Green	V21 Beige, V30 Light Green, V31 Grey
L232 Iris Blue	V1 Black, V29 Dk Blue, V31 Light Grey
L275 Light Beige	V1 Black, V16 Brown
L279 Dolomite	V1 Black, V2 Grey, V21 Beige

1955 (March–July 1955)

Exterior colour	Cabriolet hood colour options
L41 Black	V1 Black, V21 Beige, V31 Light Grey
L54 Poppy Red	V1 Black, V21 Beige, V31 Light Grey
L219 Congo Green	V21 Beige, V30 Light Green, V31 Light Grey
L232 Iris Blue	V21 Beige, V29 Dk Blue, V31 Light Grey
L316 Almond Green	V3 Green, V21 Beige
L320 Dolphin Grey Light	V1 Black
L322 Silver Granite	V31 Light Grey
L329 Shetland Grey	V21 Beige, V31 Light Grey
L370 Nile Beige	V1 Black, V16 Brown

1955–56 (April 1955–March 1956)

Exterior colour	Cabriolet hood colour options
L41 Black	V1 Black, V21 Beige, V31 Light Grey
L54 Poppy Red	V1 Black, V21 Beige, V31 Light Grey
L227 Strato Silver	V21 Beige, V31 Light Grey, V59 Dark Blue
L258 Inca Red	V1 Black, V17 Sahara Beige, V31 Light Grey
L316 Almond Green	V3 Green, V21 Beige
L320 Dolphin Grey Light	V1 Black
L329 Shetland Grey	V21 Beige, V31 Light Grey
L370 Nile Beige	V1 Black, V16 Brown
L374 Sepia Silver	V16 Brown

1956 (April–July 1956)

Exterior colour	Cabriolet hood colour options
L41 Black	V1 Black, V21 Beige, V31 Light Grey
L258 Inca Red	V1 Black, V17 Sahara Beige, V31 Light Grey
L316 Almond Green	V3 Green, V21 Beige
L320 Dolphin Grey Light	V1 Black, V2 Grey, V21 Beige
L329 Shetland Grey	V1 Black, V21 Beige, V31 Light Grey
L331 Horizon Blue	V1 Black, V31 Light Grey, V59 Dark Blue
L351 Coral Red	V1 Black, V21 Beige, V31 Light Grey
L374 Sepia Silver	V16 Brown

1957 model year (August 1956–July 1957)

Exterior colour	Cabriolet hood colour options
L41 Black	V1 Black, V21 Beige, V31 Light Grey
L241 Bamboo Green*	V1 Black, V3 Green
L258 Inca Red	V1 Black, V17 Sahara Beige, V31 Light Grey
L316 Almond Green	V1 Black, V3 Green, V21 Beige
L320 Dolphin Grey Light	V1 Black, V2 Grey, V21 Beige
L329 Shetland Grey	V1 Black, V21 Beige, V31 Light Grey
L331 Horizon Blue	V1 Black, V21 Beige, V59 Dark Blue
L336 Deep Blue	V1 Black, V2 Grey, V31 Light Grey
L351 Coral Red	V1 Black, V21 Beige, V31 Light Grey

*Available Dec '56 onwards

paint and trim colours

1958 model year (August 1957–July 1958)

Exterior colour	Cabriolet hood colour options
L41 Black	V1 Black, V2 Grey, V31 Light Grey
L241 Bamboo Green	V1 Black, V3 Green
L243 Diamond Grey	V1 Black, V3 Green, V21 Beige
L244 Moss Green	V1 Black, V3 Green, V21 Beige
L258 Inca Red	V1 Black, V17 Sahara Beige, V31 Light Grey
L329 Shetland Grey	V1 Black, V31 Light Grey
L331 Horizon Blue	V1 Black, V21 Beige, V59 Dark Blue
L338 Atlas Blue	V1 Black, V2 Grey, V31 Light Grey
L473 Alabaster Grey	V1 Black, V16 Brown

Cabriolet options were more varied than those offered for the saloon – at least in the early days. Atlas Blue and Alabaster were included in this 1958–59 Cabriolet paint options brochure.

1959 model year (August 1958–July 1959)

Exterior colour	Cabriolet hood colour options
L41 Black	V1 Black, V2 Grey, V31 Light Grey
L241 Bamboo Green	V1 Black, V3 Green
L258 Inca Red	V1 Black, V17 Sahara Beige, V31 Light Grey
L329 Shetland Grey	V1 Black, V31 Light Grey
L333 Pearl Blue	V1 Black, V2 Grey, V31 Light Grey
L473 Alabaster Grey	V1 Black, V16 Brown

1960 model year (August 1959–July 1960)

Exterior Colour	Cabriolet hood colour options
L41 Black	V1 Black, V2 Grey, V31 Light Grey
L264 Rock Grey	
L349 Jade Green	
L445 Sargasso Green	
L452 Paprika Red	
L464 Slate Grey	
L473 Alabaster Grey	V1 Black, V16 Brown

1961 model year (August 1960–July 1961)

Exterior colour	Cabriolet hood colour options
L41 Black	V1 Black, V79 Mouse Grey, V100 Silver Grey
L87 Pearl White	V1 Black
L380 Turquoise	V1 Black, V3 Green, V101 Blue Green
L390 Gulf Blue	V1 Black, V79 Mouse Grey, V100 Silver Grey
L391 Pastel Blue	V1 Black, V3 Green, V101 Blue Green
L456 Ruby Red	V1 Black, V79 Mouse Grey, V100 Silver Grey
L478 Beryl Green	V1 Black, V81 Olive Green

1962 model year (August 1961–July 1962)

Exterior colour	Cabriolet hood colour options
L41 Black	V1 Black, V79 Mouse Grey, V100 Silver Grey
L87 Pearl White	V1 Black
L380 Turquoise	V1 Black, V101 Blue Green
L390 Gulf Blue	V1 Black, V79 Mouse Grey, V100 Silver Grey
L398 Pacific Blue	V1 Black, V100 Silver Grey, V101 Blue Green
L456 Ruby Red	V1 Black, V79 Mouse Grey, V100 Silver Grey
L469 Anthracite	V1 Black, V100 Silver Grey
L478 Beryl Green	V1 Black, V81 Olive Green

1963 model year (August 1962–July 1963)

Exterior colour	Cabriolet hood colour options
L41 Black	V1 Black, V79 Mouse Grey, V100 Silver Grey
L87 Pearl White	V1 Black
L380 Turquoise	V1 Black, V101 Blue Green
L390 Gulf Blue	V1 Black, V79 Mouse Grey, V100 Silver Grey
L398 Pacific Blue	V1 Black, V100 Silver Grey, V101 Blue Green
L456 Ruby Red	V1 Black, V79 Mouse Grey, V100 Silver Grey
L469 Anthracite	V1 Black, V100 Silver Grey
L478 Beryl Green	V1 Black, V81 Olive Green

1964 model year (August 1963–July 1964)

Exterior colour	Cabriolet hood colour options
L41 Black	V1 Black, V100 Silver Grey
L87 Pearl White	V1 Black, V100 Silver Grey
L360 Sea Blue	V1 Black, V100 Silver Grey
L456 Ruby Red	V1 Black, V100 Silver Grey
L469 Anthracite	V1 Black, V100 Silver Grey
L518 Java Green	V1 Black, V100 Silver Grey
L519 Bahama Blue	V1 Black, V3 Green
L572 Panama Beige	V1 Black, V16 Texas Brown

1965 model year (August 1964–July 1965)

Exterior colour	Cabriolet hood colour options*
L41 Black	V1 Black** (Canvas only), V100 Silver Grey
L87 Pearl White	V1 Black, V16 Texas Brown
L360 Sea Blue	V1 Black, V100 Silver Grey
L456 Ruby Red	V1 Black, V100 Silver Grey
L518 Java Green	V1 Black, V100 Silver Grey
L519 Bahama Blue	V1 Black
L572 Panama Beige	V1 Black, V16 Texas Brown
L595 Fontana Grey	V1 Black

(*Canvas top replaced by Vinyl for US market)

1966 model year (August 1965–July 1966)

Exterior colour	Cabriolet hood colour options*
L41 Black	V1 Black** (canvas only), V100 Silver Grey
L87 Pearl White	V1 Black, V3 Light Sand, V671 Teak Beige
L360 Sea Blue	V1 Black, V100 Silver Grey
L456 Ruby Red	V1 Black, V100 Silver Grey
L518 Java Green	V1 Black, V100 Silver Grey
L519 Bahama Blue	V1 Black, V3 Light Sand
L568 Sea Sand	V1 Black, V671 Teak Beige
L595 Fontana Grey	V1 Black, V3 Light Sand

(*Canvas top replaced by Vinyl for US market)

1967 model year (August 1966–July 1967)

Exterior colour	Cabriolet hood colour options*
L41 Black	V100 Silver Grey
L282 Lotus White	V1 Black
L456 Ruby Red	V1 Black
L518 Java Green	V1 Black
L595 Fontana Grey	V1 Black
L620 Savanna Beige	V1 Black
L633 VW Blue	V100 Silver Grey
L639 Zenith Blue	V1 Black

(*Canvas top replaced by Vinyl for US market)

RUNNING BOARDS

Although the general impression might be that the Beetle's running boards were always covered in black rubber, nothing could be further from the case. The 1960s particularly was a time of proliferating colours. The chart below indicates the kind of variety available near the start of the decade (1961) and at the end of the period covered in this book.

Running board paint colour	Black	Sand Beige	Elf Green	Satin Blue	Glacier Blue	Citrus Yellow
Black	✓					
Pearl White		✓				
Turquoise			✓			
Gulf Blue				✓		
Pastel Blue					✓	
Ruby Red	✓					
Beryl Green						✓

By the end of the period covered by this volume, the pattern of running board colours was still reasonably complex.

Running board paint colour	Black	Savanna Beige	Fontana Grey	Zenith Blue
Black	✓			
Lotus White		✓		
Ruby Red	✓			
Java Green	✓			
Fontana Grey			✓	
Savanna Beige		✓		
VW Blue	✓			
Zenith Blue				✓

SALOON INTERIOR TRIM

Interior trim is best divided into five categories. These are: seat upholstery; door and side panels; the headlining; carpets; and rubber mats. As the majority of what follows pertains to Export or Deluxe options, it is worth noting that the general rule as far as the Standard model goes was one of spartan simplicity. For example, a Jupiter Grey Standard model of 1955 vintage would have been allocated Grey upholstery throughout, a Grey headliner, Grey-Blue carpets and Black mats. As cloth was the cheapest option at the time for seat upholstery, this was the only option offered on the Standard. (It is also worth noting that by the 1960s when vinyl became increasingly popular in both the United States and Britain, this was not generally the case in mainland Europe. As this book is primarily targeted at an English-speaking audience, the emphasis is on covering the options most likely to be found in those markets. Nevertheless, cloth seats with vinyl sides and backs were still a part of the full range in the last year covered by this book.) Although in 1955 Black mats were the only option, in other years when either Grey or Beige might have been an option, Black was deemed to be the most basic and therefore offered on a Jupiter Grey car.

On the debut of the Export or Deluxe model, all cars were allocated Beige cloth upholstery, plus door and side panels. There were two colours of headlining – Grey Beige and Honey Brown – and Volkswagen selected the most appropriate tone to complement a Beetle's external paint colour. Mats could be specified either in Beige or Black. With effect from 1950, customers could opt for leatherette instead of cloth upholstery. Leatherette was more costly at the time, but there was a second colour option, namely 'Red Beige'. From October 1952 the colour of the standard cloth interior changed from simple Beige to the more subtle Grey-Beige, although the leatherette options remained as they had been previously. From March 1953, Black was added to the choice of leatherettes, while for 1954 out went Beige-Grey leatherette to be replaced by a new option of Beige, plus Green, Grey and Slate Blue. The shade of both Green and Blue changed in March 1955, while Rusty Red was added and Beige deleted. Leatherette options blossomed, with Light Beige replacing the original shade of Beige, and Red, Grey, Blue and Green being added to the list – albeit at the expense of Black and Red-Beige. For the first time, more options were added to the choices of carpet, with Grey-Blue and Grey-Green being added to the original list of two options.

From April 1956, cloth upholstery options were revised once more, with the latest list comprising a Light Grey in addition to the older Grey, Light Beige and Copper-Red being new arrivals and Blue continuing. Leatherette options were similarly amended, with a new shade of Green and a Light Grey being added to the list.

With the arrival of the larger-windowed Beetle – complete with a new dashboard design – in the summer of 1957 for the '58 model year, the opportunity was taken to look at most options across the trim range afresh. Rubber mats were more commonly Grey rather than Black now, while all Export models were fitted with Grey-Black carpets. Headliners reverted to just two options – Light Grey and Light Beige, the one-year-plus option of Light Green (introduced in April 1956) being dropped from the listings. Most interesting of all, though, was the use of two-tone materials for both the cloth and leatherette upholstery, plus the door and side pan-els. The options immediately proliferat-ed, while it is worth reminding followers of the Standard model that such luxu-ries were not extended to this model. A chart for the first model year helps to explain Volkswagen's additional inter-est in the aesthetics of the Beetle's pas-senger compartment.

1958 model year – all cars fitted with grey mats and grey-black carpets				
Exterior colour	Cloth/vinyl seats	Door/side panels	Optional leatherette	Headliner colour
L41 Black	Blue-Grey/Blue	Blue-Grey/Blue	Blue-Grey	Light Grey
		Blue-Grey/Red	Red	
L240 Agave Green	Green-Grey/ Grey-Green	Green-Grey/ Grey-Green	Green-Grey	Light Beige
L243 Diamond Grey	Brown-Grey/ Red-Brown	Brown-Grey/ Red-Brown	Brown-Grey	Light Beige
L245 Light Bronze	Green-Grey/ Grey-Green	Green-Grey/ Grey-Green	Green-Grey	Light Beige
L334 Glacier Blue	Blue-Grey/Blue	Blue-Grey/Blue Blue-Grey	Blue-Grey	Light Grey
L335 Capri Blue	Blue-Grey/Blue	Blue-Grey/Blue Blue-Grey/Red	Blue-Grey	Light Grey
L351 Coral Red	Brown-Grey/ Red-Brown	Brown-Grey/ Red-Brown	Brown-Grey	Light Beige

By the early 1960s prioritizng of colour options had reached its peak, even though external paint colours had been rationalized more or less, at least between the Saloon and the Cabriolet.

By 1961 leatherette had more or less ousted cloth as the standard for seat upholstery. Cars painted in Black, Pearl White, Gulf Blue, Ruby Red and with effect from March 1961 both Pastel Blue and Turquoise featured Silver Beige leatherette upholstery. Ice Blue was allo-cated to these last two mentioned mod-els until March, while the final remaining colour, Beryl Green, was offered to cus-tomers with Soft Beige coverings. Car-pets and rubber mats had become more complex in the variety of options on offer, however. Rock Grey carpets were matched to Black, Gulf Blue, Ruby Red, Turquoise and Pastel Blue cars, although in the case of the last two mentioned colours, this was only the case from March 1961. Both paint options had pre-viously been allocated Malachite Green carpets, while Pearl White cars stood out with Honey Brown, as did Beryl Green cars with Olive.

To highlight the quest for perfect colour co-ordination, the Beetle with Beryl Green exterior paint epitomizes early 1960s strivings. While the car's outer wheel rims were Opal White and the inner hubs Olive Green, the run-ning board covers were Citrus Yellow. Inside, the steering column, gear stick and handbrake lever were Nepal Green, as were the steering wheel, indi-cator switch and the front passenger's grab handle. The handbrake and gear-lever boot were finished in Olive Green. The carpet was Olive Green, as were the front and rear rubber mats, plus the rear seat passengers' kick plates. The door and quarter-panel coverings were Soft Beige and Nepal Green, while the seat coverings were both Olive and Beige, in the case of the combination cloth and vinyl seat cov-erings, or Soft Beige when upholstered in leatherette.

As early as 1962 a pattern of rational-ization had started to establish itself. For example, with the sole exception of Beryl Green cars, all Beetles featured Graphite Grey carpets, as they did in both 1963 and 1964 – although by 1965 there was a change to Tin Grey on all paint options. Rubber mats followed suit with Graphite Grey dominating the 1962 listings, while by 1965 this had changed to a universal Anthracite offering. Likewise, upholstery colours had been greatly simplified, with all cars (except those with Beryl Green exterior paintwork) being offered with a Derby Grey cloth and Silver Beige vinyl trim, or in standard vinyl Silver Beige – providing the car was neither Black nor Pearl White, when the option was True Red. (Beryl Green cars were exempt from the general rule again!)

In 1964 'breathable' and striped vinyl was standard, with the majority of cars being supplied with grey materials, a few with brown and Bahama Blue cars with blue. The following year the pat-tern was the same, although the colours had been slightly amended. By far the most frequently offered was a combination of Mesh Grey and Oxford Grey, although it shouldn't be forgotten that for certain markets cloth was still an important option. Here the most likely mix of colours was Brown Grey cloth matched to Oxford Grey vinyl. There was a fairly even split in 1964, between straightforward black vinyl upholstery and Platinum, although the paintwork of a Pearl White car was nicely balanced with red seat coverings and trim. In 1967, Plat-inum and Gazelle were the near uni-versal offerings, black was offered on both Fontana Grey and Zenith Blue cars, while other colours could be specified against certain paint colours. As an example, the owner of a new Black car could choose between Plat-inum, Indian Red and Gazelle coloured upholstery. Suffice to say that refer-ence to the accompanying brochure illustrations will make the situation much clearer than ever words can.

The arrival for the 1963 model year of a 'white' perforated vinyl headlining simplified the story that had once pertained to the Beetle's headliner. In 1962 the woollen headlining for all cars was described as Silver Beige, a shade that had been universal since the disappearance of Ice Blue headlin-ers on Turquoise and Pastel Blue cars in March 1961.

CABRIOLET INTERNAL TRIM

Although the Karmann Cabriolet's trim wasn't necessarily identical to that of the Saloon, with a greater chance of more options being offered, nevertheless the two vehicles (the Deluxe Saloon and the Cabriolet) were remarkably similar. To illustrate the point, the 1950 calendar year specifications are detailed below.

1950: Saloon and Cabriolet (latter vehicle's details in *italic*)					
Trim paint colour	Cloth interior	Leatherette Interior	Headliner	Carpet colour	Rubber mats
Pastel Green	P71 Beige	K110 Beige	H108 Beige	278 Grey Beige	005 Black 071 Beige
Medium Green	P71 Beige	K110 Beige	H108 Beige	278 Grey Beige	005 Black 071 Beige
Reseda Green	P71 Beige	K110 Beige K155 Red Beige	H108 Beige	278 Grey Beige	005 Black 071 Beige
Silver Grey	P71 Beige	K110 Beige K155 Red Beige	H109 Grey	026 Honey Brown	005 Black 071 Beige
Dark Blue	P71 Beige	K110 Beige K155 Red Beige	H109 Grey	026 Honey Brown	005 Black 071 Beige
Black	P71 Beige	K110 Beige K155 Red Beige	H108 Beige	278 Grey Beige	005 Black 071 Beige
Black Cabriolet	*P71 Beige*	*K110 Beige* *K155 Red Beige*	*H108 Beige*	*278 Grey Beige*	*005 Black*
Coral Red	P71 Beige	K110 Beige	H108 Beige	278 Grey Beige	005 Black 071 Beige
Coral Red Cabriolet	*P71 Beige*	*K110 Beige*	*H108 Beige*	*278 Grey Beige*	*005 Black*
Bordeaux Red	P71 Beige	K110 Beige K155 Red Beige	H109 Grey	026 Honey Brown	005 Black 071 Beige
Medium Brown	P71 Beige	K110 Beige K155 Red Beige	H108 Beige	278 Grey Beige	005 Black 071 Beige
Medium Brown Cabriolet	*P71 Beige*	*K110 Beige* *K155 Red Beige*	*H108 Beige*	*278 Grey Beige*	*005 Black*
Beige	P71 Beige	K110 Beige K155 Red Beige	H109 Grey	026 Honey Brown	005 Black 071 Beige
Beige Cabriolet	*P71 Beige*	*K110 Beige* *K155 Red Beige*	*H109 Grey*	*026 Honey Brown*	*005 Black*
Brown Beige	P71 Beige	K110 Beige K155 Red Beige	H108 Beige	278 Grey Beige	005 Black 071 Beige
Pearl White	P71 Beige	K110 Beige K155 Red Beige	H109 Grey	026 Honey Brown	005 Black 071 Beige
Atlantic Green Cabriolet	*P71 Beige*	*K110 Beige*	*H108 Beige*	*300 Dark Green*	*005 Black*
Ivory Cabriolet	*P71 Beige*	*K110 Beige* *K155 Red Beige*	*H108 Beige*	*026 Honey Brown*	*005 Black*

As the 1960s progressed, the trim options for the Cabriolet and the Saloon became identical.

accessories

ABOVE: The contents of the Hazet spare wheel tool kit varied slightly over the years. This one – although now resident on a 1956 oval – dates from a little earlier, circa 1951.

LEFT: Here is one Kamei idea that didn't meet with approval when presented at the Geneva motor show in 1953. Although the spoiler improved the car's aerodynamics, potential purchasers gave the thumbs down on the aesthetics of the design. (Note also that the aerial is mounted across the screen and retained in position on the roof.)

RIGHT: This nifty 1964 accessories brochure, which was produced in the USA, depicts a cross-section of the most popular accessories of the day. Forty-plus years later,

As production of the Beetle curved ever upwards and Volkswagen's tentacles spread further and further across the world, so too did the number of accessories available for the car, be they officially incorporated into dealer part listings accompanied by glossy literature, or simply offered by independent firms who might well make similar items suitable for totally different makes of vehicle.

The earliest accessories of all were produced by Karl Meier, an ex-KdF worker, whose business, Kamei, gradually became synonymous with both quality and ingenuity. His furtive brain knew no limits and every conceivable extra appeared within a relatively short period of time. From the highly practical under-dash parcel shelf introduced in 1952, to items like a roof-mounted contraption for hat storage, developed in 1958, nobody could accuse Kamei of not offering a comprehensive service.

the luggage rack and the tool kit would be the most sought-after. Even such items as the rather questionable armrest and headrest had been accessory options since the start of the 1950s.

The brochure reproductions and pictures in this chapter are captioned to tell as much of the accessory story in the 1950s and 1960s as possible.

SOME OTHER VOLKSWAGEN ACCESSORIES

LOOK AFTER YOUR VOLKSWAGEN

VOLKSWAGEN

THE DICK LANE GARAGE CO. LTD.
100% VOLKSWAGEN
RETAIL DEALERS
THORNBURY, BRADFORD 64710.

ACCESSORIES

LEFT AND ABOVE: Dating from the mid-1960s, this leaflet was intended as a taster of the many options available from British dealers. Front stoneguards served little practical purpose but might harbour condensation. Should mudflaps be compulsory on all cars? In the 1950s, 1960s and beyond it was fashionable to adorn a Beetle with as much additional brightwork as possible. Some items served a practical purpose; the majority, though, simply gave a vehicle an extra Deluxe dimension.

RIGHT: The Black oval features individual anodized trim strips to enhance the air-intake slots. The same style of trim is fitted to the post-July 1957 Beetle (BELOW LEFT), while the one-piece trim (MIDDLE, BELOW), most popular in later years, is shown on a car of similar vintage.

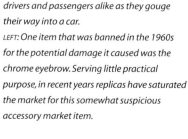

ABOVE: Not as many people went to the trouble to change the oval trims on the wing, despite the elegance of this brightwork replacement.

FAR LEFT: Rear stoneguards served the practical purpose of eliminating stone-chip damage to the paintwork on the rear wings. This large-style trim – a favourite in the 1950s – came with the built-in disadvantage of having to drill the wing before fixing the stoneguard.

ABOVE LEFT: Fingerplates varied in design as the style of door handle and more particularly the recess behind changed in shape. Although apparently something of a gimmick, compare a modern Volkswagen and the many scratches in this area are readily visible, being caused by drivers and passengers alike as they gouge their way into a car.

LEFT: One item that was banned in the 1960s for the potential damage it caused was the chrome eyebrow. Serving little practical purpose, in recent years replicas have saturated the market for this somewhat suspicious accessory market item.

ABOVE: A proliferation of badge and spotlight bars was only curbed slightly by the introduction of US nudge bars, or towel-rail bumpers. Some argue that Volkswagen never sanctioned rear wing covers (LEFT), but both overriders with rubber inserts (BELOW) and opening rear side windows (BELOW LEFT) were carried over to the years after the period covered by this volume.

Two rarely seen and certainly unofficial items are this mid-1950s 'wing' mirror (BELOW LEFT) and a rather pretentious bonnet-mounted VW badge (MIDDLE, BELOW), also shown on the car with an external visor and rear wing covers (BELOW RIGHT).

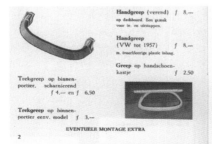

BELOW: Printed shortly after the demise of the oval-window Beetle, this tiny brochure covers sixteen pages of tightly packed options for owners. Dashboard handgrips only became standard in the 1960s, other than on the Cabriolet. Door fingerplates remained on the options list to the last days of the German-produced Beetle and beyond, but varied in size and shape according to the style of door handle fitted. Other options depicted included a windbreak for sunroof models, numerous wheel trim rings, 'silver' trim to enhance the look of the roof rain gutters, decorative trim for the twin tailpipes (known colloquially as 'cheese graters') and even a treadle-style accelerator pedal to sit over the roller fitted to earlier cars.

Huvskydd med specialfäste passande Volkswagen 1200

RIGHT: Bonnet covers were popular as they protected a vulnerable area from the inevitable crop of stone chips. However, water tended to collect behind and to the bottom of the covers, leading to rust if the cover wasn't removed on a regular basis.

LEFT: Until the arrival of a fuel gauge as a standard piece of equipment in 1962 one of the most useful accessory items was just such a thing. Beautifully engineered, even down to the inclusion of adjoining trim strips on this post-July 1957 dash, the addition of a fuel gauge avoided usage of the reserve fuel tap. However, should an owner not wish to fit one, the accessory team had something else to offer, in the form of an extended fuel tap lever (RIGHT).

BELOW LEFT: Although of no practical use, all the Beetle dashboards covered by this book could potentially sport a bud vase – such an icon of the 1950s and 1960s that when the New Beetle was launched in the 1990s a bud vase was included in the package.

RIGHT: Dating from 1966, the GHE brochure included everything from the basics to near-customized accessories. As semaphore indicators increasingly became a thing of the past, owners of older Beetles sought to replace them with modern flashing indicators. GHE provided the kit to cover the gaps left by the semaphores when removed, or to add a parking light. They also offered an unusual licence plate cover, which included reversing lights.

LEFT: Despite claims that the Beetle's heater was totally effective in the coldest of weathers, Eberspächer produced a special heater for colder climes, which could operate separately from the rest of the car, as it had its own fuel supply.

LEFT: Robert Bosch's association with Volkswagen extends back to the earliest days of the Beetle. OE (original equipment) suppliers, the company also sold everything from a battery to lower wing-mounted indicators and radios.

RIGHT: Another name synonymous with that of Volkswagen was Blaupunkt, which made radios suitable for installation into a Beetle from the days of the split-window Beetles, as depicted on the cover of this early brochure.

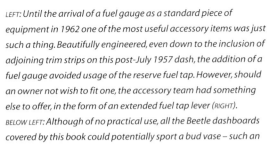

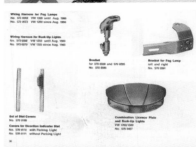

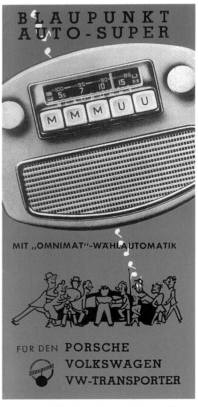

RIGHT: Blaupunkt's Blue Spot range covered just about every make of car imaginable, but there were items specific to Volkswagen and the Beetle. In this brochure dating from around 1964, Bosch showed pictures of a radio fitted to an oval and a post-1957 dashboard, as well as one designed for use in the VW 1500 (Type 3).

RIGHT: The radio shown here nestles in nothing less than a Hebmüller.

LEFT: The Judson Supercharger, which supplied the cylinders with more air and fuel than they would normally induct via atmospheric pressure, adding both extra bhp and torque, was a popular 'accessory' from the mid-1950s. Under test conditions, the Beetle's top speed – calculated to be 70.2mph (113km/h) – jumped to 83.8mph (135km/h). Equally important, the magic 0–60mph time was shaved from a sloth-like 28 seconds to just 18 seconds.

Positano, Italy.

export
'the Volkswagen is a favourite in 136 countries'

Although a few British government-inspired tentative steps had been taken to export the Beetle before the appointment of Heinz Nordhoff as Director General, in reality this more often than not was dependent on the enthusiasm of individuals to feed a car-starved market in their own country and make a considerable amount of money for themselves at the same time. The archetypal entrepreneur of those early days was the first exporter, Dutchman Ben Pon, and his story relating to both the Beetle and the Transporter quickly reveals all.

As for Nordhoff, he recognized that even with a waiting list of some 15,000 Beetles for the home market and outstanding orders for a further 7,000 cars elsewhere at the end of his first year in office, the success of the Volkswagen-werk could not be guaranteed. While the cash generated helped to repair and rebuild the bomb-damaged plant, which in turn increased both productivity and efficiency, major obstacles still lay in the way of assured success. Wary of the long, cold German winters – Wolfsburg had been closed, for example, between 6 January and 10 March in 1947 – which resulted in unhealthy seasonal peaks and troughs in home market sales. Nordhoff was also very conscious of the lack of guaranteed money with which to invest. The German government, such as it was, was in no position to assist Volkswagen financially. Nordhoff required the hard currency he would be able to raise by selling Beetles abroad and particularly from the potentially lucrative US market. On a lesser level, Nordhoff was also painfully aware that it took a German resident some 2,500 hours to earn sufficient money to afford a Beetle, while across in the United States the same person would have achieved their goal within just 450 hours.

While tentative steps had been made to upgrade the post-war Beetle, most noticeably by adding a little chrome to show models, the car remained noisy, suffered from inferior upholstery and bad springing, lacked a decent paint finish and often suffered from a short engine life. Service and parts facilities, although initiated, were not of an acceptable standard. Nordhoff was keen to rectify these crucial failings, by establishing a good distribution, dealer and parts supply network, while producing a Deluxe version of the Beetle labelled the Export model – a car that met the aspirations of markets across Europe and on the other side of the Atlantic.

FIRST EXPORTS

Spurred on by the realization in early 1947 that the British taxpayer was carrying the cost of food imports into the British Zone of Germany, it was determined that German industry should start to consider exporting to raise foreign currency to pay such bills. Although the British Control Board decided that the first countries to take Beetles should be those geographically adjacent to Germany, it was delegated to the managers to specify which should be targeted first. In 1947, fifty-six Beetles made their way to Holland. The following year this number escalated to 1,820 cars, while Switzerland received 1,380 Beetles, Belgium 1,050 and Sweden a tentative fifty-five vehicles. There was a further increase in 1949 before the programme was lost amongst Nordhoff's Export Beetle drive.

Long before the export decree arrived, Ben and Wijand Pon had tried to obtain Beetles. Their first foray had been in 1937 in the days of the KdF-Wagen – an attempt that might well have been successful if war hadn't intervened, as the Nazis always envisaged exporting their goods. In 1946, Ben Pon made his first trip to Wolfsburg but came away empty-handed. In April 1947, he was there once more, met Hirst's boss, Colonel Radclyffe, and by 8 August of the same year had a contract as the general agent for Holland. After a hitch relating to spares had been resolved, six cars (some say five) – three black and three dark blue/grey – made their way with Pon's drivers to the Dutchman's dealership. Keen to exploit the relationship, Pon also attempted to import the flatbed trucks (*Plattenwagens*) used in the factory to move goods around, but fell foul of his own country's legislation, whereupon he sketched his idea for a VW truck, which bore a remarkable

similarity to the Transporter Nordhoff would launch in February 1950.

The Swiss importer was a firm called Automobil und Motoren AG – AMAG, based in Zürich. Created as recently as January 1945, the company's concession was granted by Volkswagen on 29 April 1948. Scania Varbis took on the Swedish franchise. In Belgium, the old established coach-building firm and Studebaker franchise holder, D'Leteren, gained the Volkswagen concession in March 1948. Contracts were also signed with companies in Luxembourg, Denmark and Norway.

In 1950, one-third of the total number of Beetles produced were destined for export and the number of countries involved had grown to eighteen. By August 1955 and the occasion of the one-millionth Beetle, 700 of the daily output of 1,280 cars manufactured were for the export market and amazingly within the space of just a few years Nordhoff had increased the number of countries selling Beetles to an impressive 103. Of the first million Beetles, 400,000 cars were no longer on German soil and the percentage of such cars would continue to rise. In the most important markets strategically, Volkswagen tended to veer towards a course of setting up its own sales and customer services network. The first such was Canada, where on 11 September 1952 Volkswagen Canada Ltd was established in Toronto, Ontario. Volkswagen was at a disadvantage there, thanks to duty-free imports of British products. Nevertheless, ninety-four Beetles had been sold by the end of the year and there would be many more to follow. Volkswagen's penetration of both the American and British markets is described in detail below as an indication of both the determination and flexibility to achieve the company's goal and, as will be revealed in the next chapter, different tactics again were used to secure market share in countries ranging from Brazil, to South Africa, Australia and New Zealand.

Following France's decision to liberalize import regulations for fellow Common Market countries, Volkswagen France SA was founded in Paris on 11 March 1960, with a view to increasing market share in that country, despite the fact that in terms of imports only Fiat and Opel outperformed Volkswagen.

THE AMERICAN MARKET

Nordhoff rightly regarded the lucrative American market as crucial. Selecting Ben Pon as an ideal ambassador for the German car, Nordhoff despatched the Dutchman and a standard grey Beetle aboard the M/S *Westerdam*. Man and car arrived in New York on 17 January 1949. Apart from a wave of adverse publicity, as journalists insisted on calling the Beetle 'Hitler's car', Pon also faced a stonewall amongst potential dealers, all of whom were not the slightest bit interested in the tiny underpowered German product. Three weeks after his arrival, Pon's funds were more or less exhausted. He sold the Beetle and a collection of spares for $950 to pay his hotel bill and his fare back to Holland – hardly an auspicious start.

In April 1949, Nordhoff went to the USA himself. Ostensibly, his purpose was to attend an exhibition of German goods at New York's Museum of Science and industry. Armed with photographs of the Beetle, Nordhoff met very much the same response as Pon had done previously. As for the exhibition, which ran from 9–24 April, the second Beetle to be officially imported into the States was present, later being sold. Nordhoff later reported the trip to be an 'utter failure', although he did meet the Austrian Max Hoffman, whose European car showrooms had opened at Park Avenue and 59th Street in the heart of Manhattan in 1947.

In 1950, Hoffmann was appointed as America's East Coast VW Importer and on 10 July of the same year twenty Beetles marked for the Hoffmann Motor Company were unloaded at Brooklyn. A week later, his showroom, which was normally packed with high-powered and high-priced machinery from the likes of Jaguar and Porsche, was cleared to make way for the launch of what was described as the US premier of the Volkswagen – the 'Popular-priced West German car'. Hoffman announced to gathered journalists that his intention was to import 1,000 cars per month soon and as a definite goal to reach a rate of 3,000 per month eventually. A PR agency issued an appropriate release, indicating that the four styles of Volkswagen unveiled at Hoffman's would later be on view to the public at the First International Trade Fair in Chicago to be held

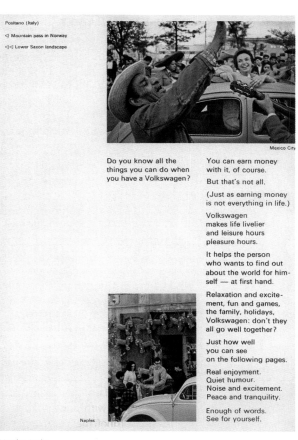

Positano (Italy)
◁ Mountain pass in Norway
◁◁ Lower Saxon landscape

Mexico City

Do you know all the things you can do when you have a Volkswagen?

You can earn money with it, of course.

But that's not all.

(Just as earning money is not everything in life.)

Volkswagen makes life livelier and leisure hours pleasure hours.

It helps the person who wants to find out about the world for himself — at first hand.

Relaxation and excitement, fun and games, the family, holidays, Volkswagen: don't they all go well together?

Just how well you can see on the following pages.

Real enjoyment. Quiet humour. Noise and excitement. Peace and tranquility.

Enough of words. See for yourself.

Naples

Naples, Italy.

Miami Beach, Florida, USA.

between 7–20 August. Prices ranged from $1,280 for the Standard model and $1,480 for the Export version, to $1,550 for the recently introduced sunroof model and $1,997 for the range-topping Karmann Cabriolet.

To Nordhoff's disappointment, Hoffman's initial enthusiasm for the product wasn't matched by that of would-be buyers. A mere 157 cars were sold in 1950, to be followed by just 390 the following year and 601 in 1952. The figure had risen again in 1953, but still only to a total of 1,237 Volkswagens. As Volkswagen sales continued to escalate both at home and in an ever-increasing number of countries abroad, Nordhoff decided to send his Export Manager, Manuel Hinke, to meet with Hoffmann and find out what was going wrong. By this time, Hoffmann had lost confidence in the product and advised Hinke that the Beetle would never sell in the USA. An agreement was duly drawn up that if sales hadn't improved significantly by the end of 1953, Hoffman's contract would not be renewed.

Nordhoff's decided that if the person he had perceived as the best importer in the United States couldn't sell the Beetle,

the only course of action was for Volkswagen's Export Department to handle matters itself. Several Americans came forward to fill the gap vacated by Hoffmann, but Nordhoff remained adamant. Gottfried Lange from the Export Department was directed to set up his office in San Francisco and a few months later in April 1954, Will Van de Kamp – a former Messerschmidt pilot and a field salesman in Germany – arrived in New York. The two men were totally dissimilar. The former was keen to set up a well-run organization based on systems with an eager and efficient network of distributors. Van de Kamp, on the other hand, was the ultimate persuasive salesman, whose interest in administrative systems was negligible.

The change in direction, however diverse, paid off and in the first year of the new regime sales bounced up to 6,344 cars. Reluctant at first to admit that he couldn't do everything single-handedly, Van de Kamp slowly acquired a growing staff and in April 1955 moved into sixth-floor offices at 720 Fifth Avenue in New York. In June 1955, Volkswagen United States Inc. was founded, with its main offices in New York.

In August 1955 a decision was taken that could well have affected the development, if not sales, of the Beetle in the USA. The merger of Studebaker and Packard gave Volkswagen the opportunity to purchase a modern, hardly used assembly plant in New Brunswick with the aim of manufacturing the Beetle in the USA. Nordhoff was only too aware that with ever-escalating sales worldwide there was a danger that he would run out of capacity. What could have been better than to build Beetles for sale in the USA in that country? A hasty decision based on somewhat suspect statistics resulted in a change of plan just six months later in January 1956. The high level of American salaries compared to the undervalued German Deutschmark then 4.2 to 1, suggested that to make a profit in America would be difficult, while to continue US production in Germany guaranteed success. Nordhoff took the decision personally to pull out of the New Brunswick project, simply stating that he had 'made a mistake'.

On 27 October 1955, Volkswagen of America Inc. was formed, which later led to the dissolution of the recently formed

Volkswagen United States Inc. Once the decision had been taken to abandon plans to build Beetles in the USA, the operation's main role became one of supervising the importation of cars, which had previously often been left to individual distributors, and to look at the overall presentation of the brand by imposing strict new service requirements. This move weeded out those dealers who chose to represent manufacturers other than Volkswagen, as they could no longer guarantee to meet the set standards. Such was the growth in business that by 1962 a new administrative building was required, while on 8 December 1964 a new plant in Emden opened, its sole purpose being to meet the demands of the North American market. Initially producing over 500 Beetles per day, within two years the assembly capacity had been increased to 1,100 vehicles daily, while the workforce had expanded from 790 to 4,487 employees accordingly.

With the acceleration of sales in the USA following the debut of Van de Kamp, Beetles bound for the United States started to be rather different animals in terms of specification and during the next decade it would be the demands of US legislation that drove the design of the Beetle forwards, culminating in a new-look Beetle for the start of the 1968 model year. From indicators rather than semaphores to special two-tier bumpers, repositioned rear licence plates and vertically set headlamps, the importance of the American market was duly recognized.

As the end of the 1950s approached, Volkswagen decided to release Van de Kamp from his contract, his style no longer being regarded as appropriate for such a large-scale operation. His successor was Carl Hahn, once Nordhoff's personal assistant and a future head of the entire Volkswagen organization in his own right. While not intended to be a fully fledged history of Volkswagen in America, it is worth noting that it was Hahn who appointed the advertising agency DDB (Doyle Dane Bernbach) to meet the challenge posed by American manufacturers contemplating production of their own small cars. Their now famous self-deprecating campaigns, unique in the world of advertising at the time, had the effect of raising the Beetle to cult status initially in the USA and later elsewhere as well. The immediate effect, however, was a decline in sales of the products of rival European manufacturers and an increase from 20 per cent to 32 per cent of the import market in 1960 for Volkswagen.

Figures semi-official and unofficial vary considerably regarding Beetle sales in the USA (*see* table *below*), but all show a continuing pattern of escalation and each acts as confirmation that Nordhoff had been right to persevere with what turned out to be his biggest export market for much of his twenty-year reign as Volkswagen's Director General.

THE BEETLE COMES TO BRITAIN

While the British were involved at Wolfsburg there were no plans to export the Beetle to Britain. At home, anti-German feeling ran high and there was also a strong patriotic belief that to buy anything other than a British product bordered on heresy. However, for Nordhoff such a situation was not acceptable, despite the fact that Britain was also known as the home of the small car, with more such vehicles continuing to be built in the UK throughout the 1950s than in any other country except Germany.

Britain's first contact with the Beetle was established by a legend in Volkswagen circles, John Colborne-Baber. He had run his own motor trade business at Ripley in Surrey for some years and by the end of the war was working on Aston Martins and Bentleys. In 1946 he sold a 3ltr Bentley to a Swedish gentleman who reappeared at his garage in 1948 with the first Beetle Colborne-Baber had ever seen. The Swedish man wished to part-exchange it for a Buick that Colborne-Baber had on his forecourt. Faced with such an unknown quantity, Colborne-Baber made a number of enquiries about the value of a 1947 Beetle, only to be met with a lack of knowledge similar to his own. Nevertheless, a deal was done, with £150 being granted in part-exchange against the price of the Buick. Colborne-Baber drove the car and was suitably enamoured with it. 'It was like a little 3ltr Bentley', he said many years later. 'The axle ratios, 3.5 to 1, were the same, the gear ratios almost the same, it had a low-revving engine – in fact, it was a small car you could drive like a sports car.' So

---

Beetle sales year by year

(source Ward's *Automotive Yearbook*; includes sales of other Volkswagens as these were introduced to the USA)

Calendar year	Sales	Alternative sales figures (Beetle only)	Number of dealers/distributors	Other information
1955	28,907		15 distributors	
1956	50,011			
1957	64,242	54,189	327 dealerships	
1958	78,261	61,507	470 dealerships	
1959	119,899			first DDB adverts released August
1960	159,995	127,159		
1961	177,308			
1962	192,570		687 dealerships	1,000,000 VW sold in USA
1963	240,143		750 dealerships	
1964	307,173	276,187	845 dealerships	
1965	371,222	314,625		sixty-five freighter ships in constant use to meet US demand
1966	427,694			
1967	454,801		930 dealerships	

impressed was Colborne-Baber that he decided to specialize in Beetles forthwith. Advertising in both *Autocar* and *Motor*, he offered to purchase the spare parts packs then being given out by Volkswagen to anyone taking a Beetle out of Germany. Inevitably, this led to buying cars as well – invariably those owned by Control Commission personnel. These Beetles, dating from the period well before the launch of the Export model, featured amongst other things hopsack upholstery and very poor paintwork. According to Colborne-Baber's own publicity machine, the cars were 'gutted, reupholstered in leather (then cheaper than Rexine, due to an anomaly in the hire-purchase laws) and resprayed. This meant that the customer could specify his own internal and external colour scheme, in fact, a custom-built Volkswagen.' By 1951, personalized Beetles were selling for £410 in LHD guise, or £425 if converted to RHD. Colborne-Baber estimated that in the region of 100 refurbished cars were sold between 1948 and 1952.

The first Volkswagen Colborne-Baber handled bore the registration number JLT 420. Sold more than once in the late 1940s and early 1950s, it reappeared some twenty years later with an additional 200,000 miles on the clock. The owner accepted £100 for the car, it was subsequently restored and has remained with Colborne Garages ever since.

During the time that Colborne-Baber was active with his refurbished Beetles, Dublin-based Stephen O'Flaherty was pioneering the Beetle's fortunes in Ireland. Having met Nordhoff in 1948, by 1950 he had been granted the honour of being the first to build Beetles outside Germany, using completely-knocked-down (CKD) kits supplied by Wolfsburg. Between 1950 and 1977, the company went on to produce a total of 72,000 Beetles.

Nordhoff decided that 'if Volkswagen is to succeed in Britain, it must be a British company under British management'. Despite having granted Colborne-Baber a licence to sell new cars in Britain in 1952 – a matter complicated by the Board of Trade, which restricted sales to foreign visitors, essentially American personal stationed at Manston Air Force Base in Kent – Nordhoff chose O'Flaherty as the man to take Volkswagen's cause forward in Britain.

The British franchise was granted on 1 January 1953. O'Flaherty brought in two partners to give his operation financial stability and by July – after a false start in June – had offices above the Lotus showrooms in Regent Street, in London's West End. A further move was inevitable though and larger quarters, including a much-needed showroom, were located on St James's Street, just off Piccadilly. (By the end of 1953 a parts department of sorts separate to the showroom had proved essential.

Again a stopgap measure, this was located in Davies Street.) Publicity surrounding the formation of Volkswagen Motors Limited had brought a deluge of people forward who wished to sell the cars, many being Jowett dealers facing considerable uncertainty as the Bradford-based company headed for bankruptcy. With 70 per cent of British production going for export at the time, further demand came from other car-starved dealers. Such was the chaos that it is fair to say that the distributor and dealership network emerged very much on an ad-hoc basis – something that was to cause problems later in that decade and the following one.

Volkswagen in Germany, tired of the interminable delay, demanded to know how many Beetles O'Flaherty and his partners wanted. Caution suggested a figure of five or ten vehicles, bearing in mind that storage facilities were non-existent, but O'Flaherty overruled his team, requesting 200 cars on the spot. As the cars were delivered from Germany they were pushed out to the distributors as quickly as possible in order that Volkswagen Motors Ltd might avoid high dock storage fees. All a distributor had to agree to was to take four cars – paying 50 per cent of the purchase price on placement of the order – and to commit to £100 worth of tools and £250 of spare parts. While this deal might have looked attractive, the discounts offered were less generous than

ABOVE: JLT 420 – probably the most famous Beetle in Britain and conceivably the first to have travelled on English roads.
LEFT: London, England.

those given by British manufacturers, which were normally between 17½ and 20 per cent. Volkswagen Motors offered no more than 16⅔ per cent.

In 1953, 945 cars were sold and Volkswagen Motors Ltd made a loss of £4,024. The company imported the Standard saloon, selling it at £649 19s 2d, the Export or Deluxe which retailed at £739 4s 2d and the sunroof model, which topped the range at £773 4s 2d. (The Karmann Cabriolet wasn't available in RHD form at this time.) With the exception of being RHD models, British Beetles were exactly the same as German models, a position that would remain more or less the case throughout the car's production run and certainly during the years covered by this volume. Admittedly, Standard models sported a little chrome – restricted more or less to bumpers and hubcaps – compared to the cars produced for the home market, while some export markets were granted cloth instead of the vinyl upholstery bestowed on British owners, but such exceptions were minor.

With a dramatic escalation of sales in 1954, financial concerns for Volkswagen Motors Ltd were replaced with difficulties in other directions. Vandalism to newly imported Beetles at Harwich docks was one issue. At its peak, three out of every four cars delivered suffered some form of damage, ranging from blows with hammers and spanners to door panels to batteries placed upside down on the floorpans, causing acid leakage. Volkswagen's worldwide success proved to be another issue, culminating in the occasion when Wolfsburg advised it was no longer able to supply any more cars for the time being due to overall demand. Volkswagen Motors Ltd sent its Managing Director – J.J. Graydon – to Wolfsburg, where he met Nordhoff, who resolved the problem by instigating Saturday working specifically to meet the demand for RHD cars. The Board of Trade's import quota system was a further issue, restricting as it did the number of cars Volkswagen Motors Ltd could import each year. When this system was finally dispensed with in 1958, higher custom duties, surcharges and additional taxes all filled the gaps to hinder maximum progress.

Against such a background, sales after 1953 were surprisingly good. In 1954, 3,260 cars were sold, while for the next two years the figure hovered at a little over 5,000 per annum. In 1958, 7,436 cars were sold and prices stood as follows. The Standard cost £653 17s 0d, the Deluxe £758 17s 0d, the Deluxe with sunroof £807 12s 0d and the Cabriolet £1,025 2s 0d. By 1959 sales had grown further, this time to 9,227 Volkswagens. This was the year that also saw the 50,000th Beetle imported into Britain – a car that was presented to the widow of Colonel Charles Radclyffe. In 1964, the 100,000th Volkswagen arrived and by 1965 sales had grown to around 28,000 per annum. Two years later, this figure had jumped to 33,000 – making Volkswagen Motors Ltd the largest importers in Britain.

In 1957, Thomas Tilling Ltd had acquired Volkswagen Motors Ltd, a move that helped to rationalize the operations activities. Nevertheless, it would be another decade before modern management techniques brought Volkswagen Motors up to the standard enjoyed by many of Volkswagen's other franchisees.

'WHY IS THE VOLKSWAGEN A FAVOURITE IN 136 COUNTRIES?'

With the change in advertising styles that took place as the 1950s gave way to the 1960s – the last Beetle brochure in the old Reuters style being produced to promote the new 34bhp engine for the '61 model year – new messages began

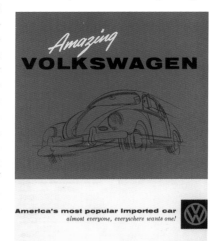

Apart from relying on Reuters' artwork and US variations within the text, in the early days simple brochures were produced virtually bullet-pointing the Beetle's assets and quoting a basic price. Black and white imagery was used on the inside fold.

to appear as well as photographic artwork. A key one was undoubtedly based around the Beetle's availability across the world in so many countries. Such a global spread had the desirable side-effect of promoting the Beetle's ability to go anywhere under any conditions. For example, the Beetle was a favourite in 136 countries because:

- 'the VW takes the steepest hills even in ice and snow'.
- 'Persistent and sturdy, it is especially popular in mountainous countries. In Switzerland, for example, Volkswagen has been the leader for years, despite a highly competitive market with more than 100 different makes of cars. Over 160,000 Swiss are enthusiastic Volkswagen owners.'

Likewise, it was a favourite because it could:

- 'nip in anywhere, even into the smallest parking space'.

and

- 'The Volkswagen has brought a refreshing new idea to car conscious America. A car doesn't have to cost a fortune, nor does it have to be a petrol-guzzling monster.'
- 'We asked our friends overseas. "Why is the Volkswagen so popular in your country? Is it because it is so different?" The answer didn't surprise us. "Yes", they said, "but not entirely. The main reason is this: pound for pound, dollar for dollar, the Volkswagen is the best buy for the money." Up to now, 750,000 Americans have bought Volkswagens. And 180,000 Canadians are driving them, too. Every year, another 200,000 in the New World are becoming enthusiastic Volkswagen owners. Nothing is harder to stop than a trend.'

Volkswagen's world coverage – its power as an exporter was clear:

- 'If fate should take you and your Volkswagen to Ruanda or Burundi someday, you'd find a friend down there already – your VW service.'

Beetles were assembled in Ireland from 1950 throughout the period covered by this book. Although virtually indistinguishable from German cars, local materials were used, as evidenced by the shamrock mark etched into the glass.

11

Beetles assembled or built *overseas*

Constant repetition of the number of countries in which a Beetle could be obtained – a hallmark of much of Volkswagen's advertising in the early to mid-1960s – extended not only to mention of sales in Switzerland and North America, as referred to at the end of the last chapter, but also to subsidiaries, which by that time were dotted across the continents.

Hence the Beetle was a favourite in 136 countries:

- 'because the VW goes on any road even where there is no road at all'.
- 'In countries where cars must operate under the severest of conditions, the Volkswagen comes out on top. Take Brazil, for example.

There, the Volkswagen is built locally. Every year 50,000 Brazilians purchase cars from our subsidiary, Volkswagen do Brasil. This is one way in which Volkswagen is contributing to Brazil's rapidly developing economy.'
- 'because the VW engine stays cool even when it's hot outside'.

Beetles assembled or built overseas

Country	Year	Full manufacture	CKD kit	Origin of CKD kit	Notes
Republic of Ireland	1950		1950	Germany	independent supplier
South Africa	1951		1951–56	Germany	some CKD kits supplied after start of manufacture
Brazil	1953	1956	1953–57	Germany	
Australia	1954	1959–68	1954–59	Germany	
Belgium	1954	1954			
Mexico	1954	1965	1954–66	Germany	
New Zealand	1954	1954–60	1960–68	Germany and, from 1960, Australia	
The Philippines	1959		1959	Germany	independent supplier
Uruguay	1961		1961	Brazil	independent supplier
Venezuela	1963		1963	Brazil	independent supplier
Portugal	1964		1964	Germany	
Peru	1966		1960	Brazil	

■ 'Take a country like Australia, for example. In places, you can drive hundreds of miles without seeing anything but kangaroos or emus, let alone people or such a thing as a garage. If you've ever wondered how reliable the Volkswagen really is, you certainly find out in a rugged country like this. Volkswagens have won five reliability trails. The courses were tough, cross-country and all round Australia. Over 10,000 miles in nineteen days and nights … Three times it has been the outright winner of the present premier Australian reliability event … This record – unapproached in Australia by any other car, regardless of size or price – is just one of the reasons why more than 120,000 Australians drive a Volkswagen today. They *need* a rugged car "Down Under".'

In the period covered by this book, Beetle assembly plants and in some cases full manufacturing operations came into being in the countries indicated in the chart above. This chart indicates each operation's status. The completely-knocked-down (CKD) kits referred to normally arrived in crates. Varying amounts of locally sourced parts would be added – these tended to include some, or possibly all, of the following: batteries, electrical items, glass and paint, upholstery, tyres and wiring. By using locally sourced materials the relevant Volkswagen operation saved on import duties, while offering support to indigenous component suppliers.

Of these, South Africa, Brazil, Australia, plus, as the years passed, Mexico were the most significant and it is to these operations that attention is turned. However, as records of the New Zealand operation have been made particularly accessible in recent years, this relatively minor assembly body has been included as an easy means of demonstrating how a CKD car might differ from one built at Wolfsburg.

VOLKSWAGEN OF SOUTH AFRICA LTD

Back in 1946, a suitable plot of land was acquired from the Municipality of Uitenhage to build a factory to assemble Studebakers. Shortly afterwards, the company behind the scheme – South African Motor Assemblers and Distributors Limited or SAMAD – had added Austins to the list. By 1951 attention had also been turned in the general direction of the Beetle, with enough parts being purchased from Wolfsburg to allow assembly of 340 cars. The first car came off the assembly line on 31 August. The following year, 575 cars were assembled, but by 1956, a time when Austins were no longer built at Uitenhage, Beetle assembly had grown to 3,000 units compared to 1,800 Studebakers.

On 12 October 1956, in a move described as one of consolidating its position, Volkswagenwerk GmbH acquired a 38 per cent interest in SAMAD, increasing this to 57.6 per cent the following year. During 1956, the first steps were taken towards full manufacture, with the installation of body panel presses, while a couple of years later a foundry was also functional. CKD continued unabated, while Volkswagen also resorted to shipping in complete cars to counteract the worst effects of a waiting list for a Beetle of between two to three years.

By 1964 the South African operation was producing over 19,000 Beetles annually, following closely any changes in specification coming out of Wolfsburg. In November 1966 the company was renamed as Volkswagen of South Africa Ltd with Volkswagenwerk AG owning a 63 per cent interest. Government demand that 55 per cent of all manufactured models should be of South African origin spurred Volkswagen to further action.

Realistically, South African produced Beetles differed little from their German counterparts. Local content ensured that items like headlinings varied from the norm at Wolfsburg, but for many it would be difficult to identify a 1960s Beetle of South African origins as opposed to a German-built car. As a country driving on the right, one anomaly is worth a mention. For a period of two years, the Uitenhage factory was assembling RHD split-window Beetles – a rare occurrence indeed.

VOLKSWAGEN DO BRASIL

As early as 1949 there was an interest in the Beetle in Brazil. José Thompson, the Chrysler importer for Brazil at the time, convinced the firm's president, C.T. Tomaz that the Beetle was the right car for Brazil. Nordhoff was duly contacted and he visited the country, accompanied by Dr F. W. Schultz-Wenk. In co-operation with Chrysler and supported by a 20 per cent local investment, Volkswagen established Volkswagen do Brasil on 23 March 1953, assembling Beetles from imported parts from day one. Over the next four years a workforce of 200 assembled in the region of 2,800 cars. Full manufacture began in September 1957 at a new factory near São Paulo, but until 1959 the Transporter was the only vehicle on the production line.

Plates indicating CKD kit manufactured in Germany and assembled in South Africa (South African Motor Assemblers).

Local content – 'ribbed', plastic-based headlining.

The South African Beetle pictured – dating from 1960 – is one assembled at Uitenhage from a kit. By this time, cars were being manufactured, assembled and imported from Germany to cope with the demand.

RIGHT: All South African cars include reflectors, front and rear.

Beetles were assembled in Australia from kits supplied by Wolfsburg from 1954 until 1959, when full manufacture started. This car dates from 1957 and bears a remarkable resemblance to all German-built cars – other than the paint colour, unique to Australia.

When the Beetle joined the manufacturing process local content had risen to 95 per cent of the total. Brazilian vehicles came to differ significantly from their German counterparts as the years passed. Perhaps one of the most notable changes not to be implemented in Brazil was the increase in glass size affecting all German-made Beetles built for the '65 model year and onwards. Likewise, kingpins were retained after their demise in Germany. By 1966, the Brazilian operation was turning out 95,000 Volkswagens of all types per year, supplying other Latin American countries with kits to build their own Beetles and accounted for over 60 per cent of all cars sold in Brazil, as well as 42 per cent of Brazil's total motor vehicle production.

Year	No. of Beetles manufactured in Brazil
1959	8,383
1960	17,059
1961	31,025
1962	38,430
1963	42,362
1964	51,755
1965	59,996
1966	77,624
1967	91,821

VOLKSWAGEN AUSTRALASIA PTY LTD

Although the first Beetle to descend upon Australia was a 1946 model, the year was 1951 and it would be a further two years before the importation of cars began officially. Faced with something of a mixed reception for the Beetle, Regent Motors (Holdings) Ltd, Volkswagen's nominated importer as of October 1953, nevertheless negotiated with coach-builders Martin and King Ltd to assemble CKD cars for them in Clayton, a suburb of Melbourne. The first shipment of CKD kits arrived in June 1954 and by the end of the year 1,385 cars had been assembled. The following year this figure had grown considerably to 6,634 Beetles. Local content became increasingly important: in 1956 it stood at 51 per cent, by 1958 at approximately two-thirds and by 1959 this had further increased to 75 per cent of the car's make-up.

As a direct result of a visit by Nordhoff, Volkswagen (Australasia) Pty Ltd was formed on 6 December 1957 – its aim was to manufacture Beetles and other models using locally sourced parts. The Volkswagenwerk owned 51 per cent of the shares and in 1958 the subsidiary acquired all the stocks of the former authorized importer, which then assumed responsibility for service. In January 1959, manufacture began in a much-expanded factory, which had cost a great deal to effect. The move to full production with body panels being pressed took place in 1962. In 1963, the operation added the preparation of replacement engines to its portfolio. In 1964 the Australian government demanded production should be 95 per cent local content by 1969. Production costs proved high and capacity levels weren't met. Competitors seemed capable of producing cheaper models designed especially for the Australian market. As a result, Volkswagen lost market share, its sales plummeting in 1966 from the previous year's figure of 34,588 to just 19,586 models of all types. The highest single year's sales of Beetles was in 1964, when 25,736 cars were sold.

Initially, Australian Beetles were difficult to distinguish from their German counterparts except that a whole range of items, including paint, glass, tyres and electrics, were sourced locally. However,

Virgin forest near Acapulco, Mexico.

after 1961 the Australian-manufactured Beetle stood in something of a time warp. Thus at the end of the period covered by this volume, an Australian Beetle did not benefit from the larger window glass introduced in Germany in 1965 or ball joint suspension, which followed a year later. The 1300 engine arrived a year later than in Germany, while the 1500 engine was still absent at the end of the '67 model year.

VOLKSWAGEN MEXICANA

Following the establishment of Volkswagen Mexicana in January 1954, the first Mexican dealership opened and by the end of the year 618 vehicles had been sold. Nine years later, in 1963, there were nearly forty distributors and annual sales had grown to 6,378. In 1960, Volkswagen Mexicana had changed its name to VW Interamericana. In August 1962, the Mexican government decreed that the only manufacturers to receive production licences would be those who had managed to achieve 60 per cent local input. As a result, VW Interamericana opened its own assembly plant – Promexa. Previously, Mexican Beetles had been assembled from German CKD kits by Studebaker Packard de Mexico and

Valle del Bravo, Mexico.

Mexico.

from 1961 by Chrysler Automex. VW Interamericana recognized that if it was to gain or even retain its share of the Mexican market, substantial investment would be required by Volkswagen in Germany. A threat from the Mexican government to restrict the number of manufacturers and models competing for custom spurred the decision and on 15 January 1964 Volkswagen de Mexico, SA de CV was established as a wholly owned subsidiary of Volkswagenwerk AG. In 1965 sales increased by 59 per cent and the decision was taken to open a new production site in Puebla, which opened in November 1967 utilizing locally manufactured parts in full accordance with the Mexican government's demands.

Throughout the period covered by this book Mexican Beetles were virtually indistinguishable from those produced at Wolfsburg, differences only emerging with the '68 model.

VW MOTORS NEW ZEALAND – FORMERLY JOWETT MOTORS

Trading under the name Jowett Motors, thanks to their lengthy association with the marque, the Turner family,

who had been in business since 1937, acquired the Volkswagen franchise in December 1953. On 11 January 1955 the company name was changed to VW Motors, New Zealand and shortly afterwards plans were laid to develop a purpose-built factory for the assembly of Beetles, a project that was completed in 1958 at a time when the company was under considerable financial pressure. Revised government import allocations meant that the company was limited regarding the number of Volkswagens it could build and had to turn to assembling other manufacturers' cars to ease the financial pressures. Assembly of Volkswagens had started in 1954 in premises previously used to assemble Jowetts. The first kits were despatched from Germany in April 1954, arriving in New Zealand in July. Most of the panels required welding, while it was expected that items such as tyres and glass could be sourced locally and were therefore excluded from the CKD crates.

It was in the interests of VW Motors, New Zealand to attempt to source as many parts as possible locally. The greater the local content, the larger the import licence that could be obtained.

In 1959, New Zealand's Department of Industry and Commerce granted an import licence for 1,000 cars and 200 Transporters on the proviso that the following parts were manufactured in the country: 'Starter cables, earth straps, shock absorbers, wheels, muffler, plastic mouldings for door panels, rubber mouldings for doors, bonnet and door rubber, floor mats, running boards, rear-view mirror, sun visor, looms and all wiring, seat spring assembly, seat covers, paint and headliners.' By 1962, local content had grown to $37\frac{1}{2}$ per cent.

By 10 May 1962, 10,000 Beetles had been assembled in New Zealand, but a change was afoot. Despite massive investments, at the beginning of the 1960s Wolfsburg could still only fulfil around 85 per cent of the demand worldwide for Beetles, while its attentions were already being diverted by the arrival of the VW 1500, or Type 3. As a result, it was decided that VW Motors, New Zealand would be supplied with kits prepared in Australia (1962: 12; 1963: 900; 1964: 1,704; 1965: 1,752; 1966: 2,004; 1967: 1,296). In May 1964, the company became a public one and was renamed Motor Holdings.

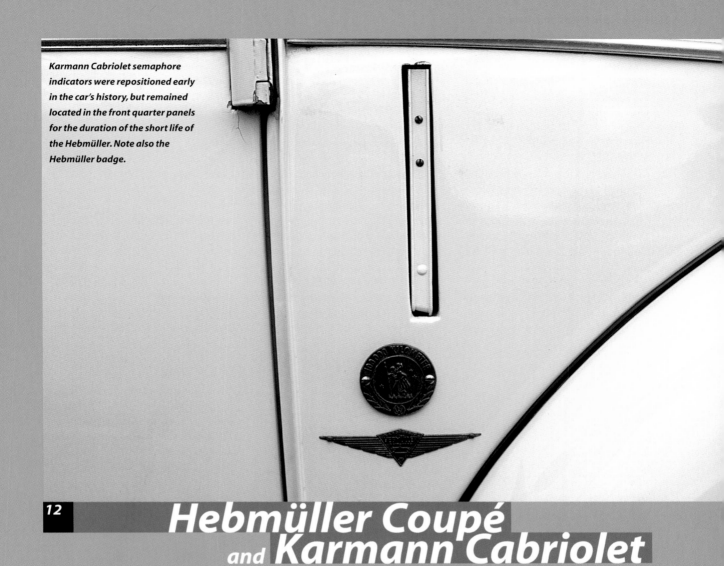

Karmann Cabriolet semaphore indicators were repositioned early in the car's history, but remained located in the front quarter panels for the duration of the short life of the Hebmüller. Note also the Hebmüller badge.

12 Hebmüller Coupé and Karmann Cabriolet

That both Porsche and his Nazi bosses always intended a convertible version of the Beetle is amply shown by the photographic records of the era. As early as 1936 the first prototype Beetle, the V1, had been joined by a soft-top version of the car, the V2, and this vehicle was tested extensively alongside the standard saloon. Numerous images of Ferry Porsche, son of the designer and future head of post-war Porsche, at the wheel survive. The V2 was later rebuilt, emerging as the convertible example in the W30 series of *Versuchwagens*, or experimental cars. Few could have failed to notice pictures of the convertible KdF-Wagen at the factory foundation-laying ceremony in May 1938. Perhaps even better known are the images of Hitler in the passenger seat of a soft-top KdF-Wagen. Wishing to be seen by the masses, the convertible KdF-Wagen served the dual purpose of bringing

the Führer to the people and reinforcing the message that the Nazis were creating transport for all in what had been previously a country starved of cars for all but the most wealthy. Hitler's convertible – the foundation-laying ceremony car had later been presented to him on the occasion of his fiftieth birthday – survived the war and a claimed 600,000km (372,840 miles). Suitably restored, it is now an exhibit in the museum at Wolfsburg.

With the Nazi regime swept away, Porsche in exile and the British in charge at Wolfsburg, perhaps it was fortuitous that Ivan Hirst too had a fascination for open-top motoring and sufficient spare manpower to allow the infant experimental department to build a new convertible Beetle. Such one-off soft-top models are discussed in the next chapter.

With the arrival of Heinz Nordhoff, the situation could so easily have

changed. Here was a man with a mission to see Volkswagen spearhead Germany's economic revival. His master plan for the future security of Volkswagen was to conquer the world's automobile market with a version of the saloon designed to entice buyers. Although enthusiastic about a convertible version of the car, Nordhoff was less then convinced that Wolfsburg should devote precious time to the building of such a niche-market model. For many years to come, demand for the Export Beetle would outstrip supply many times over. The factory had to concentrate on building saloons. Fortunately, two companies had more than a passing interest in taking the problem away from Nordhoff's hard-pressed hands.

All Volkswagen had to do was supply the body panels and mechanical components, market the product as a luxury add-on to the general range and offer an aftersales service, which it would have been unheard of to refuse. The two companies with a desire to take up this challenge were Hebmüller and Karmann, both of which had already been active in the field of prototype soft-tops.

THE HEBMÜLLER COUPÉ

The coach-building firm of Hebmüller and Sohn was founded in 1889 in the town of Wuppertal in Germany's southern Ruhr. Before the war and after the death of the company's founder Joseph, the four Hebmüller sons had come to specialize in the production of both Cabriolet and luxury versions of products made by well-known names such as Ford and Opel, with others including Hanomag and Hansa-Loyd.

With the Allies in charge of occupied Germany, the British commissioned Hebmüller to build 15 cabriolets using a Humber chassis.

Keen to be involved with a soft-top luxury version of the Beetle, Hebmüller produced design drawings, all of which were clearly influenced by the Radclyffe Roadster (*see* next chapter). Nordhoff's appointment was sufficient to ensure that work on prototypes might begin, but contrary to the often-repeated statement that Beetle chassis were made available at this point, all three prototypes produced in 1948 were based on cars built in 1945 or the earlier months of 1946, as evidenced by pictures showing round jacking points – a characteristic of such early vehicles.

Perhaps inevitably the prototypes carried many features not destined to be a part of the production run. These included use of the Saloon's 'Pope's nose' brake light and number-plate light housing, plus air-intake slots carefully cut into the engine lid.

The biggest problem relating to all three prototypes was the near inevitable one of body flexing. Doors were soon misaligned and the Saloon's windscreens retained in the design of the prototypes cracked as the hoods were clipped back into place after an open-top drive. A slightly redesigned surround with more squared-off corners and crucially the inclusion of a heavy tubular frame into this surround, plus a substantial steel plate welded

LEFT: This car is one of three prototype Hebmüllers. Note the round jacking points and the unique hubcaps.

BELOW: From the front this 1950 Hebmüller is virtually indistinguishable from a Karmann Cabriolet; however, from the rear it's a totally different story. Undoubtedly the specially 'moulded' engine lid cover is the car's most endearing panel.

across the base of the windscreen (and visible from the car's boot) were sufficient to solve the problem at the time the pre-production car was built in April 1949. General body flexing was remedied much in the same way that Karmann tackled the problem. The sills were strengthened by the attachment of heavy box-section metal welded underneath, while adding panels alongside the front seat occupants' legs reinforced the bulkhead. At the rear a pair of boxed reinforcing panels adorned the engine compartment, side panels and strengthening plates were welded inside the car and a hefty cross-member was added under the rear seat.

The pre-production car was subjected to a gruelling programme of tests that included being driven on the roughest of roads for some 10,000km without ill effect. As a result, Wolfsburg granted full approval, placed an order for 2,000 cars and bestowed upon the Hebmüller the type designation 14. Series production began in June 1949.

What Hebmüller had created was undoubtedly the most aesthetically balanced and beautiful Beetle, even though the car came with a built-in penalty in the form of the rear seat, which was clearly only intended for occasional usage. Although the carefully designed aluminium-framed side windows were unique to the car and the fact that the hood stowed away completely flat and behind the rear seat when down, it was at the Hebmüller's back where it really came into its own. The wonderful contours of the elongated engine lid at first sight appeared to be a straightforward copy of the standard boot lid, whereas in reality it was a carefully crafted hand-formed panel. Its crowning glory was the inclusion of a long scoop-like pressing that housed the number-plate light. Unlike the Karmann, there were no disfiguring slots cut into the engine lid by the time the Hebmüller went into full production – the air intake louvres being positioned between the lid and the hood – a position made possible by the fact that with the top down no metalwork was obscured. Careful use of aluminium trim – extended to the engine lid – and a wide variety of paint options – including the very much in vogue two-tone combinations – completed the picture of perfection.

Many Hebmüller owners opted for side panels finished in contrasting colours. Perhaps the main option on this 1949 Hebmüller isn't the most restrained, but it does demonstrate that early Volkswagens and their derivatives weren't necessarily all sombre in appearance.

Finished in Ivory, this Hebmüller looks fine apart from the large window in the replacement hood – the cars featured in the other pictures have the correct style of hood, however restricted visibility was.

Unlike that of the Karmann Cabriolet, the Hebmüller's hood folded completely away, affording excellent rearward vision for the driver.

The first Hebmüllers cost 7,500DM, although in 1950 the price was reduced to 6,950DM, a pattern that no doubt would have been extended in the 1950s – as with other elements of the Beetle range – if the Hebmüller Company had survived. On 23 July 1949 a fire broke out in the paint shop and spread to part of the production area before it could be brought under control. A section of the factory roof collapsed, damaging machinery and destroying partly completed cars. Although Hebmüller were producing cars within four weeks of the Saturday afternoon fire and indeed as the chart to the right indicates, were to complete much higher numbers per month than previously, the incident somehow gnawed at the roots of the company. Whether it was because the cause of the fire was never satisfactorily explained, or possibly due to inefficient, ineffective management is not clear, but Hebmüller's financial support slowly but surely weakened, culminating in the withdrawal of promised funds in early 1950 and production grinding to a halt in April. In 1952 Hebmüller declared itself bankrupt, remaining production already having been transferred to Osnabruck and Karmann.

Production figures for the Hebmüller Type 14A Coupé (or Cabriolet)			
Year	Month	Number	Notes
1948		3	prototypes
1949	April	1	pre-production
1949	June	27	
1949	July	28	fire, 23 July
1949	August	24	
1949	September	17	
1949	October	39	
1949	November	104	
1949	December	119	
1950	January	125	
1950	February	100	
1950	March	77	
1950	April	17	
1951	August	1	made by Karmann
1952	May	12	made by Karmann
1952	December	1	made by Karmann
1953	February	1	made by Karmann
Total Coupé production		**696***	

* Although the official figures from Volkswagen clearly total 696, the original figure issued was given as 750 cars.

THE KARMANN CABRIOLET

In 1954, Nordhoff said of Karmann and its Cabriolet version of the Beetle that Volkswagen was 'in genuine co-operation to supply a genuine demand, whose existence we acknowledge, but which our output does not allow us to satisfy'.

By this time, annual Beetle production stood at a figure of 202,000 units and was due to continue to increase steeply as every year passed. From the 364 Cabriolets produced in 1949, Karmann's production had grown to 4,740 units five years later. Although further escalation was near inevitable, the massive leaps and bounds experienced by Volkswagen in general did not extend to the Karmann Cabriolet. The slightest hint of recession hit Cabriolet sales hard – for, after all, it was much more of a plaything than any other element of the Beetle range would even pretend to be, while the price differential between the Saloon and the Cabriolet reflected the amount of hand-finished work dedicated to the latter, despite the fact that many of the components were supplied by Wolfsburg.

After the war, Karmann approached the British for the go-ahead to produce a soft-top version of the Beetle. Founded in 1874, the coach-building company started in business by producing horse-drawn carriages. Taken over by Wilhelm Karmann in 1901, by the following year the company was given its first commission to build a body for a motorcar and one year later the decision was taken to concentrate on this kind of work. At the start of the Second World War Karmann employed 600 people, but after severe bomb damage the situation changed dramatically. Reduced to producing such essentials as wheelbarrows,

One of a series of well-known publicity shots of the Karmann Cabriolet dating from 1949.

Wilhelm Karmann – who died at the age of eighty-eight in 1952 and who was succeeded by his son of the same name – was determined to clamber his way back to coach building. Sadly, as a German not only did he need an official permit to obtain a Beetle body and chassis on which to work, but also he was restricted to repair work rather than fully-fledged coach building.

Not to be deterred, Karmann was eventually granted a Beetle. Legend has it that this was the 10,000th model to be produced after the war. Having been given the go-ahead to produce a prototype convertible, two coachbuilds followed in relatively rapid succession. The first lacked a rear window, sported external hood hinges and came minus an ability to wind down the rear side windows. The second version saw progression in that concealed hinges and the flexibility of wind-down rear side windows were both concealed into the design. However, both cars were subject to a greater or lesser degree of flexing, an inevitable result of hacking the roof off the Saloon and despite the vehicle's separate chassis with its considerable backbone.

Karmann eventually overcame this issue by adding strengthening members under the sills, a redesign of the front quarter panels and substantial reinforcements around the bottom of the two doorframes. The inevitable penalty was a hefty increase of 44kg (97lb) in weight over and above that of the Saloon and the consequent effect on the car's already modest performance.

Nordhoff's appointment as Director General in January 1948 and the currency reforms of the same year led Karmann to push for a third prototype – a car that made its appearance in May 1949, only to be rapidly followed by twenty-five pre-production models. Each of these cars was put through a difficult test programme, amounting to a total distance covered per Cabriolet of 20,000km (12,428 miles). The report produced after the test period came to an end on 5 August 1949 concluded that here was a car well worthy of a VW badge. Later in the same year Nordhoff presented Karmann with an order for cars, generally accepted to be 2,000 in number – although some argue for a lower figure of 1,000; however, production had already begun on 3 June 1949 at a rate of

Despite later additions – the most obvious being 1960s style indicators – this Cabriolet dates from 1952. All pre-1958 model year Cabriolets can be identified by the two sets of vertical air-intake slots.

This very original Cabriolet can be dated as a pre-October 1952 example, the bumpers and tail lights both being excellent dating clues. The all-glass window in the hood was little more than a slit in the early days.

Two blocks of eighteen vertical air-intake slots – from start of production to the end of the 1957 model year.

Two examples of earlier Cabriolets.

one and sometimes two cars per day. By the end of the year this tally had increased to six. Nordhoff's only stipulation was that original Volkswagen components must be used if possible.

Designated the Type 15, production of the Karmann Cabriolet involved a reasonable amount of work – certainly not just a question of slicing the Saloon off at the waistline. To maintain some degree of body rigidity a hefty cross-member was welded into the area under the rear seat. The sills were reinforced by large box-section supports, while the front quarter panels were adapted from the inside with the inclusion of double-walled panels. Although both the boot lid and the wings were straightforward Saloon panels, the engine's cover had to be adapted to accommodate air inlets – the Saloon version's under the rear window slots being lost by the design of the Cabriolet's hood. Two blocks of eighteen vertical slots, one on either side of the backbone of the engine lid, were standard for a good number of years, before finally giving way to two blocks of five horizontal slots for the 1958 model year.

The vast majority of changes made to the Cabriolet were merely a reflection of Volkswagen's general policy of continually improving the Saloon. It is worth noting that when Volkswagen uprated the Beetle's engine size – specifically here relating to the introduction of the 1300 and 1500 – the general rule was that the range-topping Cabriolet would be offered with the largest engine option available. Very early models featured semaphore indicators standing proud on the 'A' pillar forward of the car's two doors. A change came at the end of 1949, with relocation to a position below the trim line and behind the doors. This move was forced by a need to strengthen the metalwork near the windscreen.

Virtually unprecedented for a soft-top – certainly in the price bracket of the Karmann Ghia – the window at the rear of the hood was made of glass. Starting production with what amounted to little more than a slit in the hood, in October 1952 the area of glass was increased, while in 1957 for the 1958 model year a further increase occurred, this time amounting to 47 per cent. At this point, just as the Saloon's front screen increased in size, so too did the Cabriolet's – by 8 per cent, while the surrounding pillars were made narrower.

As for the hood, here was a masterpiece designed to be sufficiently robust that a Cabriolet could be kept outside all year without adverse results. The frame was made of a combination of steel and wood. For many years, the roof liner was made of fabric, this eventually changing at the time the Saloon's headlining altered from cloth to PVC. The outer, consisting of appropriately treated linen, protected a combination of rubberized fabric mixed with horsehair, which was

The early style of Karmann badge, used until July 1960.

The later and more ornate Karmann badge introduced August 1960.

ABOVE: Although the Cabriolet was always recognized as being a cut above the rest of the Beetle range, Reuters bestowed upon it an opulence that reality couldn't quite match. Note particularly the flowing lines of the wings – the rear one curves beautifully into the valance – plus seat backrests more suited to an open-top Bentley.

LEFT: Reuters pitched the Cabriolet towards lady drivers.

A clutch of later Cabriolets dating from 1963, 1964, 1965 and 1967 respectively. Note the larger hood window, which arrived for the 1958 model year.

TOP: *For once, Reuters' interpretation of the Beetle's lines doesn't work quite so well – this brochure dates from the late 1950s.*
ABOVE: *Compare this drawing of the Cabriolet with the hood down with the one shown on page 117. Not only has Reuters changed the dash to the post 1957 style, but he has also revised the engine compartment lid to incorporate the 'new' horizontal air-intake slots.*
RIGHT: *Dating from the mid-1960s this posed photo still tells the Cabriolet's story well.*

Why is the Volkswagen a favourite in 136 countries?

The success of the Volkswagen all over the world is unique in the automotive industry. What are the reasons for the VW's popularity?
Although a fast and comfortable car, the Volkswagen is so truly economical that people can afford to own it. Although many other cars offer some of its advanced technical features (engine in the rear, or air cooling, or independent torsion bar suspension), the Volkswagen combines all of these features so sensibly, that people in 136 countries drive it with enthusiasm.

Although this car's record goes back over 15 years, today the VW is still years ahead of its time. A sane business policy has resulted in the continued improvement of a product that was good, right from the start.
Although it is, of course, an imported car in all of these countries, the Volkswagen has never been sold where VW workshops and parts depots had not been established first.

The Volkswagen comes in three different models:
(1) The Volkswagen De Luxe Sedan (shown on these pages).

guaranteed to both keep out the weather and to achieve a result where the Cabriolet with its hood up was as quiet as the Export model Saloon.

Paint options different to those of the Saloon were on offer for a number of years and invariably were of a more luxurious nature visually (*see* Chapter 8).

Likewise, the occasional trinket – such as the passenger dash-mounted grab handle added in May 1954 – would become standard on the Export model a few years later. Glancing at a selection of Cabriolet brochures dating from the mid to late 1950s, Volkswagen, as the provider of marketing skills, was careful

to describe and illustrate a wide variety of accessories that could adorn the Cabriolet. These included a clock added next to the single dashboard gauge, armrest cushions to match the upholstery, whitewall tyres with 'high polish metal beadings', as well as a variety of 'touring fitments' and covers.

Production Karmann Cabriolet versus Saloon with selected price comparisons				
Year	No. built of Cabriolet	No. built of Beetle	Cost DM of Cabriolet	Cost DM of Export Beetle
1949	364	46,146		
1950	2,695	81,979	6,950DM	5,700DM
1951	3,938	93,709		
1952	4,763	114,348		
1953	4,256	151,323		
1954	4,740	202,174	6,500DM	4,850DM
1955	6,361	279,986		
1956	6,868	333,190	5,990DM	4,700DM
1957	8,196	380,561		
1958	9,264	451,526		
1959	10,995	575,407		
1960	11,921	739,443	5,990DM	4,740DM
1961	12,005	827,850		
1962	10,129	876,255		
1963	10,599	838,488		
1964	10,355	948,370		
1965	10,754	1,090,863		
1966	9,712	1,080,165		
1967	7,583	925,787		

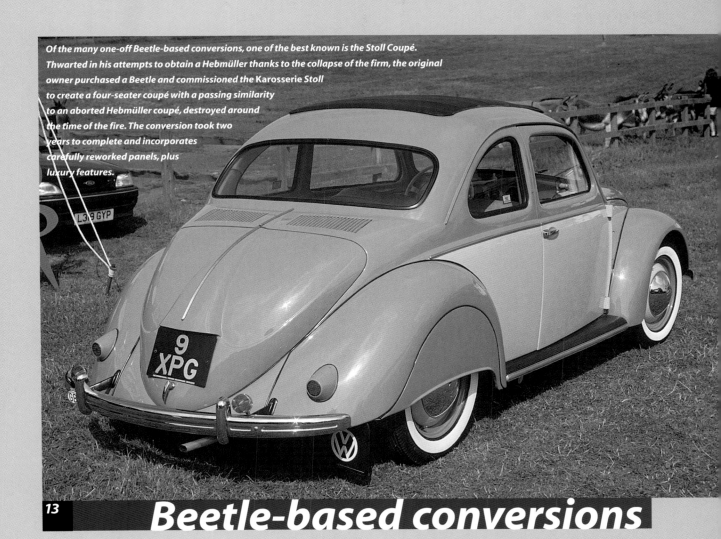

Of the many one-off Beetle-based conversions, one of the best known is the Stoll Coupé. Thwarted in his attempts to obtain a Hebmüller thanks to the collapse of the firm, the original owner purchased a Beetle and commissioned the Karosserie Stoll to create a four-seater coupé with a passing similarity to an aborted Hebmüller coupé, destroyed around the time of the fire. The conversion took two years to complete and incorporates carefully reworked panels, plus luxury features.

Beetle-based conversions

13

INTRODUCTION

Primarily thanks to its separate chassis, the Beetle proved to be an ideal vehicle on which to build a whole variety of bespoke bodies. Both Karmann and Hebmüller, as discussed in the previous chapter, had received the official sanction of Volkswagen to build their Cabriolet and convertible Coupé respectively. Their products were actively marketed and promoted through the VW sales organization and indeed it was intentional that to the buying public's eyes that they were perceived as an integral part of the Volkswagen range.

EXPERIMENTAL WORK AT WOLFSBURG

Inappropriate to the chapter covering Karmann and Hebmüller, nevertheless the experimental work carried out at Wolfsburg in the period of British control merits mention, if for no other reason than that one long since scrapped car has lived on in the minds of enthusiasts – this vehicle apparently being the inspiration for the Hebmüller.

Although it might be assumed that the last thing on the minds of Major Hirst and his team at Wolfsburg in 1946 would be development or experimental work, this was far from the case. Under the tutelage of the highly skilled mechanic and panel beater Rudolph Ringel, a member of the original Porsche team, a small number of men allocated all their time to developmental work. During a slack period, Ivan Hirst suggested the building of a soft-top Beetle. Ringel took a saloon, removed its roof, tidied up the windscreen surround – nevertheless leaving the curved top to the screen glass – improved the car's now weakened rigidity by adding stiffeners along the sills, plus across the car's rear, under the rear seat, and the job was done. This full four-seater, canvas-hooded vehicle – complete with two little windows replicating the saloon's split-rear window –

was used either to convey Hirst to meetings, or for him to drive when on Volkswagen business. An additional role was one of demonstrator, when visitors came to the factory.

According to some sources, more than one such convertible, or 'chop-top', was built and archive photographs seem to confirm this, as amongst other evidence the design and position of the respective cars' semaphore indicators varies. As a concept, the chop-top Cabriolet was fundamentally flawed. While a second row of cooling louvres stamped in the engine lid to the same layout as those below what would once have been the rear windows looked aesthetically unattractive, the surround of the windscreen was weak, resulting in frequent instances of cracked glass as the hood was repeatedly secured and unsecured from the metalwork.

Following an aborted attempt by Colonel Michael McEvoy to convince Hirst of the need for a Volkswagen-based sports car, a further task emerged for the experimental department. Hirst conceived the notion of a two-seater cabriolet, once again based on the saloon. Although adverse to the concept on the grounds of the panel beating involved, Ringel and his team set about the creation of what was undoubtedly the forerunner for the design of the Hebmüller Coupé. A boot lid was adapted at Hirst's suggestion to provide a graceful engine lid cover, the overall effect being one of an aesthetically attractive and balanced car. Trimmed with an unprecedented amount of chrome work for the era, its engine boosted at least for a time with twin carburettors and generally exuding quality, Hirst offered summer use of the coupé to his commanding officer, Colonel Charles Radclyffe. The car quickly became known as the Radclyffe Roadster – a term that has remained in popular usage ever since.

Factory records infer that a second Roadster was constructed. However, the consensus is that following an accident involving a steel girder, when Radclyffe's driver was at the wheel, the damage caused to the chassis frame, clutch housing and crankshaft was such that it was best resolved through a replacement chassis – hence the potential confusion.

UTILITY VEHICLES

The Wuppertal, or more precisely Wülfrath-based, firm of Hebmüller, the Cologne coachbuilders Papler and the former Austrian branch of the Czech Tatra firm, Austro-Tatra, all built soft-top utility versions of the Beetle for police usage. After the war, most police fleets consisted of a motley collection of former *Wehrmacht* vehicles, cars that had been requisitioned during hostilities and vehicles that had previously belonged to the occupying forces. Curiously, while the Beetle was selected ahead of others for police usage, forces chose to opt for open-topped four-door conversions. Gradually, as the 1950s unfolded, the conversion of standard saloons to police soft-tops fell out of favour and the cars built were replaced by Karmann Cabriolets. Official Volkswagen figures reveal that 2,105 basic versions of the Karmann Cabriolet were handed over to the police up to 1960, while after that year

The Radclyffe Roadster – a product of the experimental department in the days of British control at Wolfsburg and a car that bore a striking resemblance to the later Hebmüller.

use of the Cabriolet appears to have been restricted more or less to the riot police.

HEBMÜLLER

The Standard Beetle formed the basis of Hebmüller's conversion, although the work required was extensive. After removing the roof, all the window surrounds were likewise dispensed with; at prototype stage attempts had been made to retain the Standard saloon's rounded-off windscreen surround, with no success. The new strengthened window surround acted as a fixing point for the hood. In order to achieve as little chassis flex as possible, box-section strengtheners were welded around the heater channels and the sills, while under-sill strengthening rails were added. Thanks to these, the door openings could be of a realistic proportion. Although the majority of Hebmüllers for police usage were specified with four canvas flaps instead of doors, a smaller proportion featured specially fabricated steel doors with removable windows. The fabric hood was unlined and very loose fitting, but it did fold right back, affording maximum visibility to all the car's occupants. Later versions of the Hebmüller conversion lacked the standard saloon vents below what would have been the rear window so that the hood would fold even further out of the way. However, new vents had to be cut into the engine lid to compensate for this loss and while the majority were similar to those on the Karmann Cabriolet, a few cars were produced with circular holes cut into the engine lid.

The interior of the Hebmüller police car was more or less the same as the Standard model and included black dashboard fittings and the ubiquitous three-spoke steering wheel. All cars were painted Pine Green, although the finish varied between matt and gloss according to the vehicle's intended purpose. All cars lacked any form of chrome trim. Built between 1948 and 1952, accurate production records weren't kept, but at least one author has suggested that a grand total of 482 cars were produced. Each cost 5,900DM, just 900DM more than the Standard model at the time. Considering the amount of work required it might be considered that the various police forces involved got a very good deal.

FRANZ PAPLER

Well-known in coach-building circles for its elegant conversions on both the Rolls-Royce and Mercedes chassis before the war, difficult trading conditions after the conflict induced Papler to turn its hand to other things, including building vehicles based on the Volkswagen Beetle for police usage. Compared with the Hebmüller, the Papler's hood was both better designed and more substantial in nature. Even more importantly, all Paplers featured steel doors and these were of a better fit than those of the Hebmüller, where employed. The Papler's design encompassed a squared-off windscreen surround and glass similar to that of the Karmann Cabriolet. However, the metalwork was considerably more bulky. Each Papler conversion took approximately two months to complete, with great attention being paid to details such as additional grab handles fitted for the use of rear-seat passengers. Although the vast majority of the Paplers built were for police usage, a few found their way into the hands of fire departments. Such cars were painted red rather than green.

There were three firms producing soft-top Beetles for police usage. These cars are all by Papler, the Cologne-based operation.

AUSTRO-TATRA

Although the exact number of conversions carried out by Austro-Tatra isn't entirely certain, records seem to indicate a figure between 203 and 319 cars produced between 1950–51. There were 150 cars definitely destined for the Vienna force and many of these vehicles saw service until the end of the 1950s. Similar in appearance to the Papler, the Austro-Tatra design incorporated metal doors, albeit ones that were less well executed in their design. Some cars featured wide front doors compared to those at the rear, while all rear-seat passengers sat higher than was the norm with the Standard saloon. The canvas hood was similar to that produced by Hebmüller, in that part of the hood frame was exposed. Some cars incorporated the air-intake louvres below the Standard car's rear windscreen, while others had slots cut into the engine lid. Another variation came when Austro-Tatra built some of

the cars to have a fixed roof at the front and a folding rear section. Porsche Konstruktionen GmbH in Salzburg handled the business.

MIESEN

Miesen, a coach-building company based in Bonn and founded in 1870, converted its first Volkswagen (a Type 82E – the Beetle with a Kübel chassis) into an ambulance in the latter years of the war. This practice continued after hostilities and well into the era dominated by VW's Bus, at least in terms of ambulances, only ceasing in the early years of

the 1960s. Apparently, by this time close on 500 such vehicles had been built. The front passenger seat was dispensed with, as was the rear bench seat, while the passenger door was adapted to open much wider than was normal. This facilitated the manoeuvring of a stretcher, loaded onto a platform, which in turn was swivelled so that the patient lay alongside the driver. A new rear seat was installed, with a split backrest, so that when the stretcher was in use, someone could still sit close by and administer the necessary assistance until such point that the patient arrived at his or her destination. A dog-legged gear lever was amongst the modifications made to the car to ease the practicalities of this most unusual conversion. The Miesen Krankenwagen also featured a large box arrangement with a canvas top to it on the car's roof.

Various operations attempted to produce a delivery van version of the Beetle. While Porsche had conceived something that bore a close resemblance to a saloon with a garden shed lodged in its rear, some of the later options looked

Various companies, including the Belgian firm of Meeussen and the reasonably well-known Swiss operation, Beutler, produced 'vans' or 'estate versions' of the Beetle. The examples reproduced here, both of which appear to be the work of the latter mentioned firm, date from the 1960s – a time when most had already ceased production of such models, primarily due to high selling prices.

reasonably attractive. However, while the Beetle's engine lay at its rear, available loading space, the impracticalities of hoisting goods up and over the engine and the inherent inaccessibility of the engine for even routine servicing made the Volkswagen a less than perfect vehicle for such conversions. Principal among the van producers were Meeussen of Belgium and Beutler of Switzerland. This latter firm's conversion included ingenious roll-down sides, which sadly also went to highlight the lack of storage room available – starting as it did over and above the line of the top of the rear wing.

COACH-BUILT CARS UTILIZING THE BEETLE'S CHASSIS

The cluster of firms and their vehicles outlined below, together with the many other operations ranging from one-man, one-off conversions to successful coachwork operations, failed to benefit from the advantages bestowed on Karmann and Hebmüller. Indeed, Volkswagen positively discouraged many of the coachworks responsible for some truly attractive pieces of machinery. For many years, Volkswagen was extremely reluctant to sell a bare chassis to anyone who hadn't had their product sanctioned at Wolfsburg. Neither was this the doing of petty-minded minor officials at Wolfsburg. The instruction came from the Director General, Heinz Nordhoff. His thinking was flawless. In an age when however Wolfsburg tried to meet the demand for the Beetle it failed, why 'donate' much-needed parts to small concerns that hadn't either tried or been successful in their endeavours to seek approval from Volkswagen for their designs.

At a press conference held in 1954 Nordhoff was asked specifically about coachbuilders who made applications to be supplied with chassis. Nordhoff's reply was clear-cut: 'This is a car factory not a chassis factory. We wish to retain control of the appearance of cars that carry the company name. Simple supply of chassis is of no interest to us whatsoever.'

The majority of the coach-built models based on the chassis of the Beetle were intended to satisfy the growing demand in an increasingly prosperous or buoyant post-war Europe for exclusivity, or at least for hand-built cars with

The Dannenhauer and Stauss featured 'suicide' doors. Later examples had a one-piece windscreen, while general Beetle updates such as a change in dashboard style and bumpers were incorporated into the conversion.

design and looks as their main point of interest. Such cars inevitably weren't cheap and in several instances this factor led to either a decision to cease production, or the demise of the company as a coachbuilder.

DANNENHAUER AND STAUSS

A former employee of Reutter, the company involved in amongst other things the production of the VW38 or prototype KdF-Wagen, Gottfried Dannenhauer teamed up with his son-in-law, Kurt Stauss, to form a new Stuttgart-based coachworks, trading as Dannenhauer and Stauss. The year was 1950 and their goal was to produce a Beetle-based cabriolet. Turning to two of the leading stylists of the day, Wagner and Oswald, the new company soon received a design concept, which bore more than a passing resemblance to a Porsche 356.

Unlike many other coach-built cars, the Dannenhauer and Stauss had a steel body and as each was hand-built, no two cars were entirely the same. The doors were rear-hinged; the exterior trim level, while not entirely minimalist, was certainly not garish either. Early cars featured a split-panel windscreen, although a single curved glass later replaced this. Although by far the majority of D&S models produced were cabriolets, a few coupés were built for customers too.

Inside, the dashboard was pure Beetle and was updated to reflect changes made by Wolfsburg – hence in October 1952 the D&S acquired the dash associated with oval Beetles. The seats were

both designed and trimmed by the company, as no VW seats were either available or appropriate. Although suitable for four adults or two adults and three children, rear-seat passengers would have had an uncomfortable ride on little more than sparingly padded wooden boards. A bonus, however, was the hinged backrest, which opened to allow access to additional luggage space in the void between the cab and the engine. A hood comparable in terms of quality with those offered by Karmann lacked one vital ingredient. Instead of glass, at least with the later cars produced, the D&S featured a plastic window which was sewn into the hood. More modern than the Beetle, flashing indicators were fitted to the car from the start, although some cars were issued without the rear fittings. All owners were intended to use the back-up semaphores provided.

D&S struggled, as did many other unofficial converters, to acquire the essential Beetle chassis. Wolfsburg was careful to avoid their availability, leaving D&S the unenviable task of scrounging a few chassis from the local VW dealer,

while others came from far and wide, a few even being brought back to Stuttgart from as far away as Volkswagen's Swedish importer, Scania Vabis. Eventually, in the early months of 1955, Wolfsburg decided to make more bare chassis available, but by this time another problem was looming on D&S's horizon. Always considerably more expensive than the Standard Beetle even in both Export and Cabriolet guises, D&S owners paid a hefty premium over that asked for the Karmann Ghia, which was launched in the summer of 1955. Taking between 800 and 1,000 hours to build, the D&S was simply too expensive and in 1956 production ceased.

ROMETSCH

Founded in 1924, the Berlin-based coach-building firm of Freidrich Rometsch found a major source of pre-war income in the building of taxis, invariably based on either a chassis from Opel or Ley. Post-war, Rometsch, like many others, was keen to receive any form of commission in an attempt to rebuild the business. In late 1951, a four-door Beetle specifically for taxi-owner usage was announced. Although 18cm (7in) longer than the Standard saloon, amazingly the weight difference was limited to just 25kg (55lb). Developed by Johannes Beeskow, the taxi's creation involved the dismantling of a saloon, cutting through the roof panel just behind the doors and welding an additional panel in place. Pillars for the extra doors were added, returning in the process a degree of rigidity to the car once more. To fully accommodate the new doors, not only were the originals made shorter, but also the rear quarter panels were cut back and diminutive rear side windows added. The chassis of the taxi was likewise cut and then stretched, the backbone being duly reinforced. The conversion cost 2,000DM, exclusive of the trappings of the taxi trade, which included both a meter and light. The conversion's popularity resulted in many being built, the design being robust enough for owners to achieve high mileages and for the car to enjoy longevity.

Johannes Beeskow was also responsible for the design of the Rometsch vehicle that has been known for many years by the less than flattering name of the 'Banana', thanks to its length and particularly its curvy shape. Launched at the 1950 Berlin Motor Show, although it was mechanically identical to the Beetle on which it was based, that was where any similarity ended. Its length of 4.40m (14.4ft), compared to the Beetle's 4.07m (13.4ft), and 1.58m (5.2ft) width put side by side with the saloon's 1.53m (5ft), the weight differential was an inevitable 800kg (1,764lb) against 712kg (1,570lb) for the Export model. Available as both a cabriolet and a coupé, early 'Bananas' can be identified by their two-piece windscreens. The 'Banana' received a facelift in 1954 with the introduction of a single-piece curved windscreen and an enlarged rear window. Wind-down side windows and a simplicity of trim – more or less restricted to a single polished metal strip along each side of the car, plus one running down the engine and boot lids respectively – were amongst the car's characteristics. Substantial bumpers afforded adequate protection against parking knocks, while across the car's nose and above the rear licence plate chrome mouldings added to the design thanks to their substantial nature. The 'Banana's' doors extended to the bottom of the sills and when opened revealed hefty strengthening members. Design-led metal contours over the front wheels more or less completed the exterior appearance, although it is worth noting that the headlamp units, the indicators and rear-light clusters were not Volkswagen products. Rear-hinged doors were amongst the 'Banana's' idiosyncrasies. Initially utilizing the dashboard panel characteristic of the pre-October 1952 Beetle, later 'Bananas' had their own dashboard style, although usage of the Beetle's instruments remained extensive. The cars were three-seaters, with access to the single rear seat being available by tipping the front seat backrests. The single rear seat was fitted across the car and could be folded away when not in use to make way for more luggage.

In 1957 a new Rometsch was launched. Designed by Bert Lawrence, most perceived that the car had been built with the American market in mind. Featuring a wraparound windscreen, a large rear window and what might best be described as a pinched waist, the car was also notable for its large, circular, multi-purpose rear lights – all echoing the offerings from Detroit. Constructed out of aluminium over a frame of steel and wood, each car took the best part of 1,000 hours to build. Whereas the earlier model tended to be powered by a standard Beetle

These photographs show a Rometsch taxi of 1953 vintage. The addition of doors – giving easy access to the rear seat – increased the overall length of the vehicle by approximately 18cm (7in).

engine, the new car invariably received an uprated power plant in the shape of an Okrasa conversion developing 50bhp, with a top speed of 140km/h (87mph). Initially only available as a cabriolet, a coupé joined the line-up later, although neither variant achieved the acclaim allocated to the earlier design. Rehashed in 1960 with most of the more garish aspects of the car swept away, the building of the Berlin Wall in 1961 deprived Rometsch of most of its skilled workers as they were now resident in the East German sector. Rometsch ceased to operate as a coachbuilder in 1962.

This later model – 1954–57 – Rometsch roadster, known by enthusiasts as the 'Banana', can be distinguished from the earlier models by its one-piece windscreen and specially designed dashboard. Note how the doors extend to the bottom of the sill, and the car's lights, which weren't taken from Volkswagen's stock

BEUTLER

Beutler was a Swiss concern based at Bern; like Dannenhauer and Stauss, it lacked a lengthy pedigree as a coach-builder, having been established just after the war in 1946. Initially more closely associated with Porsche, as Beutler produced special-bodied 356 models, when Porsche moved from Gmünd to Stuttgart the company lost its right to continue with such models. Having tinkered with both pick-up Beetles, of which a reasonable number were built but none have survived, and ones with a plexiglass roof panel, Beutler was ready to launch a Beetle-based sports car in 1954. Available as both a cabriolet and a coupé, the latter having the edge in terms of appearance, Beutlers were built

to order. Modern and stylish but not outlandish, the Beutler had great appeal.

With a body hand built of aluminium, stressed bulkheads resolved problems of rigidity, while the doors lacked frames around the windows and were of generous proportions, allowing easy access to all seats. The rear seat was split, allowing the stowage of additional luggage as necessary, while all were specially built by Beutler and trimmed in either cloth or imitation leather according to a customer's requirements. Although

additional instrumentation could be specified, a Beutler in basic form came with the Beetle's single gauge, plus both fuel and oil temperature gauges, a cigarette lighter and a non-Volkswagen steering wheel, most usually made by Petri. Most were fitted with the standard 30bhp engine of the day, but a Porsche 356 engine could be specified. Like Dannenhauer and Stauss, Beutler experienced great difficulty in acquiring the necessary supply of Beetle chassis to meet customer orders.

The coupé was revamped in 1957, with the new version offering less pronounced rear wings and revised trim for the body. Surprisingly, two styling versions of the car were available, one with a small front grille designed to appeal to the European market and the other with a larger, wider grille and finned rear wings destined to satisfy those with a preference for American styling.

DREW

Founded in 1938, the Drew *Karosserie* moved to Wuppertal in the Ruhr in the immediate post-war period. The brothers – Gerhard, Erwin and Werner – produced their first so-called sports car in 1948. At least when viewed from

Lacking the attractive styling of the earlier Rometsch models, the new 1957 roadster was designed with the American market in mind. Initially only available as a cabriolet, a coupé quickly followed. The model was revamped in 1960 – the main effect being much less chrome.

above, the car was decidedly box-like or square in shape. Swept-back wings and Beetle headlamps were more or less overshadowed by bold usage of heavy trim, which was epitomized by the heavily ridged, specially made bumpers and a host of equally prominent brightwork trim at the car's front. Even the panes of the split front windscreen were surrounded by a heavy and visibility-restricting trim strip.

Despite giving the appearance of being a much larger car than the Beetle, due to substantial overhangs at both its front and rear, interior space was somewhat limited. Certainly, the rear seats were unsuitable for anyone larger than the average child, while the luggage space available in the boot was somewhat difficult to utilize to full effect. Quality interior trim, which included the option of purpose-built luxurious seats instead of the standard Beetle ones, gave the car a certain air, although Beetle owners would have been familiar

with the dashboard instrumentation and even the glovebox.

The aluminium-bodied car took on average in excess of 1,000 hours to build, with the result that the Drew was a costly piece of machinery, inevitably restricting potential sales to all but the privileged few. Sadly, by the time production ended in 1951 sales had failed to break above the 150 barrier.

OTHER COACHBUILDERS

Space precludes detailed references to the many other coach-built cars based on the Beetle. However, amongst the many others, a brief mention of a few outstanding examples is worthwhile. Tuscher of Zürich adapted Beetles to offer an almost cabriolet-like lifestyle for owners, by removing the roof in its entirety to the point below the rear window and replacing the missing metal with canvas. Although a competent operation, the former saloon Beetle

lost a great deal of its rigidity. Denzel in Austria built a Beetle-based sports car, which bore a passing resemblance to the Porsche 356. Enzmann of Switzerland's car was unusual in that the body was made of fibreglass, rather than the much more normal for the time aluminium. Apart from increasing the car's chances of longevity, the lightweight nature of the body ensured that the Beetle's 30bhp engine didn't feel too sluggish.

THE KARMANN GHIA

The type designations for Wilhelm Karmann's beautiful Karmann Ghia Coupé launched in 1955 and the Cabriolet version that followed in 1957 (for the '58 model year) instantly reveal the origins of the vehicle. If a LHD Standard model Beetle was the 111, an Export car a 113 and a Karmann Cabriolet a 151, the Karmann Ghia slotted nicely between as a 141 and 143 in Cabriolet and Coupé form respectively. That the two cars – the Karmann Ghia and the Beetle – shared a mechanical pedigree is apparent. As an example, when the Beetle progressed from a 30bhp engine to a 34bhp unit, so too did the Karmann Ghia. However, to describe the Karmann Ghia as a coach-built version of the Beetle is nevertheless unfair, despite the number of man-hours it took to build and the degree of hand-finishing required. The Karmann Ghia – the sheep in wolf's clothing – was a model in its own right, an essential element of the Volkswagen family, albeit built by Karmann. This beautiful car merits a volume of its own – but a passing reminder of its origins doesn't go amiss here.

ABOVE: The only known surviving Drew – styling varied over the production run of around 150 cars, each taking up to 1,000 man hours to build, but all were somewhat clumsy and slab-sided in appearance.

RIGHT: Conceived in 1953 and entering production in 1956, the Enzmann 506 – built close to Lucerne in Switzerland – featured a futuristic fibreglass body. Lacking doors, in order to give the body strength, stepping scoops (just visible in this photograph) were a part of the design, affording relatively easy access to the specially made bucket seats. A padded dash was another attribute of the interior, while a substantial air scoop at the car's rear made the design look modern more than ten years into production. Most owners opted for an uprated engine, but even with the standard VW unit of the day, the 506 performed reasonably well, thanks to its overall weight of around 550kg (1,213lb).

bibliography

Barber, Chris, *Birth of the Beetle* (Haynes, 2003)

Bobbitt, Malcolm, *Volkswagen Beetle Cabriolet* (Veloce, 2002)

Copping, Richard, *Volkswagen – The Air-Cooled Era in Colour* (Veloce, 2005)

Copping, Richard, *VW Beetle – The Car of the 20th Century* (Veloce, 2001)

Coyle, Philip, *50 Years of Volkswagens in New Zealand* (Transpress, 2004)

Cropsey, Bob, *Volkswagen History to Hobby* (Jersey Classic Publishing, 2004)

Etzold, H.R., *The Beetle – Volume 1 Production & Evolution* (Haynes, 1988)

Etzold, H.R., *The Beetle – Volume 2 Design & Evolution* (Haynes, 1990)

Etzold, H.R., *The Beetle – Volume 3 Beetlemania* (Haynes, 1991)

Fry, Robin, *The VW Beetle* (David & Charles, 1980)

Garwood, J.T., *Volkswagen Beetle – The Car of the Century – Vol. 2 1961–1980* (J.T. Garwood, 1986)

Glen, Simon, *Volkswagens of the World* (Veloce, 1999)

Gunnell, John, *Standard Catalog of Volkswagen 1946 – 2004* (K.P. Books, 2004)

Kuch, Joachim, *Volkswagen Model History* (Haynes, 1999)

Ludvigsen, Karl, *Battle for the Beetle* (R.B. Bentley Publishers, 2000)

Meredith, Laurence, *Original VW Beetle* (Bay View Books, 1994)

Miller, Ray, *Volkswagen Bug – The People's Car* (The Evergreen Press, 1984)

Nelson, Walter Henry, *Small Wonder – The Amazing Story of the Volkswagen* (Hutchinson & Co., 1970)

Parkinson, Simon, *Volkswagen Beetle – The Rise from the Ashes of War* (Veloce, 1996)

Price, Ryan Lee, *The VW Beetle* (H.P. Books, 2003)

Railton, Arthur, *The Beetle – A Most Unlikely Story* (Eurotax, 1985)

Sloniger, Jerry, *The VW Story* (Patrick Stephens Ltd, 1980)

Seume, Keith & Shaill, Bob, *Volkswagen Beetle Coachbuilts and Cabriolets 1940 –1960* (Bay View Books, 1993)

Volkswagen, A.G. (ed.), *Volkswagen Chronicle Vol. 7 Historical Notes* (Wolfsburg, 2003)

Wilson, Bob, *The 1949 – 1959 VW Beetle* (Beeman Jorgensen, 1994)

index